ISBN 978-1-5281-2535-2
PIBN 10899006

This book is a reproduction of an important historical work. Forgotten Books uses
state-of-the-art technology to digitally reconstruct the work, preserving the original format
whilst repairing imperfections present in the aged copy. In rare cases, an imperfection in
the original, such as a blemish or missing page, may be replicated in our edition. We do,
however, repair the vast majority of imperfections successfully; any imperfections that
remain are intentionally left to preserve the state of such historical works.

1 MONTH OF
FREE
READING

at

www.ForgottenBooks.com

By purchasing this book you are eligible for one month membership to ForgottenBooks.com, giving you unlimited access to our entire collection of over 1,000,000 titles via our web site and mobile apps.

To claim your free month visit:
www.forgottenbooks.com/free899006

ECONOMIC AND SOCIAL DEVELOPMENT OF RILEY COUNTY UNTIL

THE COMING OF THE RAILROADS AS REFLECTED IN

THE NEWSPAPERS

by

GOLDA CHARLENE LA SHELLE

A. B., University of Nebraska, 1929

A THESIS

submitted in partial fulfillment of the

requirements for the degree of

MASTER OF SCIENCE

KANSAS STATE COLLEGE
OF AGRICULTURE AND APPLIED SCIENCE

1931

TABLE OF CONTENTS

INTRODUCTION

History of Kansas Newspapers, 1859-1866

This study was undertaken with the purpose of investigating the economic and social development of Riley County to the coming of the railroads in 1866. The material was chiefly gathered from Riley County newspapers, *The Western Kansas Express*, the *Manhattan Express*, and the *Manhattan Independent*, also the *Leavenworth Times* and the *Topeka Tribune*, though only occasional reference to Riley County was found in the two papers last mentioned. Other sources used were A. T. Andreas, *History of the State of Kansas*, William E. Connelley, *History of Newspapers* and his book, *Kansas and Kansans*, Daniel W. Wilder, *Annals of Kansas* and several volumes of the *Kansas State Historical Collection*, along with the first Secretary's book of the Manhattan Town Association.

The *Western Kansas Express* was the first newspaper ever printed in Riley County, or west of Topeka, in Kansas Territory. It was first published in Wyandotte (Kansas City, Kansas) in May, 1859, and the plant was later brought by steamer up the Kansas River to Manhattan.[1] The first

_____

1. Andreas, *History of the State of Kansas*, p. 1307.

issue of record is for August 20, 1859 at Manhattan.[1] The
Italian refugee, Mr. Charles F. de Vivaldi became the
editor and played a dominant part in the life of the community. His influence through his newspaper and his other
activities carried great weight and had much to do with
shaping the early history of Riley County. He was one of
the best educated and most influential men in the Territory. He continued as editor of this paper until 1861,
when President Lincoln appointed Mr. de Vivaldi consul to
Santos, Brazil.

On September 17, 1859 the heading of the paper was
changed to the Manhattan Express because it did not do
full justice to those who felt most interest in Manhattan.
It had been made the official paper of the city of Manhattan and Horace Greeley in recommending it to his readers
called it the Manhattan Express.[2] The editorial in the
first issue made known that it was strictly Republican [3]
in policy and since it was the only paper, it became the
official Republican organ in Riley County.[4] This policy
continued as long as the paper existed. It was published
every Saturday morning and carried the following card.

1. William E. Connelley, History of Kansas Newspapers,
        State Printing Plant (Topeka, Kansas, 1916) p. 276.
2. Manhattan Express, September 17, 1857.
3. Western Kansas Express, August 20, 1859.
4. Manhattan Express, January 5, 1861.

Western Kansas Express
Charles de Vivaldi Editor——————Proprietor
One copy one year $ 2.00
Payment in all cases in advance
The paper to be discontinued at the expiration of the
    time for which payment has been made
Single copies, done in wrappers, 10 cents each
Rate of advertising:

One square inch,	one insertions———	$ 1.00
" " "	three months———	$ 4.00
" " "	six months———	$ 6.00
" " "	one year———	$ 8.00
¼ column	six months———	$ 20.00
	one year———	$ 30.00
½ column	six months———	$ 35.00
	one year———	$ 55.00
1 column	six months———	$ 60.00
	one year———	$100.00	1

In the winter season of 1859 and 1860, wood and
occasionally feed stuffs were accepted as payment. Calls
were made repeatedly asking for wood, even going so far
as to say that if the paper was to be printed, wood must
be brought in. The editor could not get the wood and
issue the paper. During this period the paper was published very irregularly and frequently only a half sheet,
due to a shortage of paper and the condition of the roads
which made it impossible to go to Leavenworth to obtain
more.[2] In one instance the paper was delayed due to roads
being closed and no mail service for ten days.[3] This
notice appeared in the issue of the Western Kansas Express

1. Western Kansas Express, August 20, 1859.
2. Hamilton Bureau, August 14, 1860, Ibid., June 2, 1860
3. Kansas Kansas Bureau, January 25, 1861.

August 17, 1861. "To our subscribers; the last few weeks
we have been obliged to issue half a sheet. The hard
times, a consequence of the last year's drouth has been
felt by us. The greater portion of this years subscrip-
tion, though the year is nearly passed, remains unpaid,
and a large part of the first years subscriptions."

In 1860 a new job power press that would print "every
discription of posters, bill heads, circulars, cards,
checks, books, pamphlets, and catalogues. Also printing
in prints and colors," was added to the equipment of The
Express.[1] In January, 1861, through the Leavenworth Times,
the Western Kansas Express became connected with the tele-
graphic dispatch and according to declaration, was able to
furnish news a few days in advance of many of the Eastern
newspapers.[2]

From 1861 to 1863, the Manhattan Express continued
under the editorship of Mr. James Humphrey. In 1863 it
was purchased by Mr. J. H. Pillsbury and called the Manhattan Independent. This paper continued until 1866 when
it was sold to L. R. Elliot.

On July 18, 1866, another paper, The Kansas Radical

1. Manhattan Express, April 21, 1861.
2. Ibid., January 5, 1861.

was started by R. C. Manning. This paper was purchased by L. R. Elliot in 1868 along with the Manhattan Independent and the two were consolidated into the Manhattan Standard.

It is chiefly from these papers that the material for this thesis was secured. The organizations of these papers was very similar. Before the war, the front page of each paper was usually given over to advertisements, a short story with a very pointed moral, a "Just For Fun" column and perhaps a poem which was the work of some local novice. All legal suits of non residents were run for six weeks before being brought to trial and a notification of all trials was published.[1] There was a great deal of interest, especially in Vivaldi's paper, in governmental affairs. The issue of December 17, 1858 had a column headed "Congressional Seandals" in which various members of Congress were critized and exposed in a manner similar to that of our own day. Party platforms were always given a prominent place. Foreign affairs also received considerable space and comment. Here it was most interesting to watch Italian dominance in European

---

1. Manhattan Express, September 24, 1858.

affairs as seen by the local paper.

Notifications of taxes and delinquent tax lists were
always published.[1] Every issue carried a column from the
New York Tribune urging people to send in subscriptions
to "Horace Greeley Company." Above all of these various
interests advertising was supreme until the war. One
half of the paper was usually given to war news and the
other half to advertising, with occasionally a brief
column of Personals.

The law of the newspapers was to be found in every
issue. Local correspondence is found among various newspapers and letters from all over the country were received and published.[2] There appears to have been a
great deal of rivalry between the editors of Junction
City and Manhattan, and Mr. Vivaldi is criticized quite
severely for a "pollywog" edition of his paper.[3] In one
issue the Junction City editor vigorously attacked the
Manhattan Express calling it a "Best Machine" having at
its mast-head an Italian refugee.

Until the war, agriculture was given due attention
in the newspapers. Articles were copied from the Prarie

1. Manhattan Express, February 1, 1860.
2. Ibid., October 1, 1860.
3. Kansas Tribune, September 1, 1860.

Banner, St. Lawrence Journal, and Prayer Journal. A
farmer's department was maintained.[1] During the early
part of the war this was dropped, but was revived again
in 1862.[2]

In the last years of the war 1864-1865 and immediately following, the attention of the people was turned to
the closing campaigns and to reconstruction. It seemed to
be the absorbing topic constantly before the people and it
was in this reconstruction period that the railroads began
to appear.

CHAPTER II——THE SETTLEMENT OF RILEY COUNTY

The first annual report of the trustees to the stockholders of the Manhattan Town Association disclosed that
the town site of Manhattan, as was surveyed by them in
1855, or at least "a portion of it was selected as a suitable place for a town by G. S. Park, Esq., as early as
June 1854, and that in November of the same year Mr. Park
erected a cabin, it being the first building raised on
what is now regarded as the City site. The name chosen by
Mr. Park was Polesam (also spelled Polestro and Polestia)

_____

1. Manhattan Express, May 23, 1861.
2. Ibid., March 11, 1862.

compounded of two Greek words meaning central city. Mr.
Park spent the following winter in Texas and did not return to this place until April 1865." 1 He was the first
white settler known to have located in Riley County.

Riley County was the western-most county in Kansas,
having the Kansas River as the southern boundry, as organized by the territorial legislature of 1855. Its northern
boundry was Marshall County and its western, "the line between ranges five and six east; its eastern boundry, Cal-
houn County, lying east of the line dividing ranges ten
and eleven east." 2 What was then settled and really
looked upon as Kansas, was northeastern Kansas. From
1857 to 1873, various changes were made in the county
lines of Riley. The part of it east of the Big Blue is
now the major portion of Pottawtomie County. The western
boundry of Riley was extended eight miles west from the
lines dividing ranges five and six. Davis County had
been enlarged by territory taken from Riley and Riley had
in turn had additions from the counties of Davis and
Wabaunsee. This was accomplished by a town meeting held
at the court house in Manhattan. "Riley County received

1. Secretary's Book, Manhattan Town Association. Copy of
   Secretary's Report.
2. Andreas, Op. Cit., p. 1300.

its name directly from the military post of Fort Riley,
and indirectly from General Benjamin Riley, an officer of
the United States Army." [1]

On July 31, 1852, Col. T.T. Fauntleroy, of the First
Dragoons, while in Washington, D. C. in a letter to Major-
General T. S. Jessey, Quartermaster-General of the United
States Army, urged the establishment of a military post
at or near a point on the Kansas River, where the Re-
publican River unites with it. [2] He also recommended that
Forts Leavenworth, Scott, Atchinson, Kearney and Laramie
be discontinued and all troops concentrated at the proposed point. In the autumn of 1852, Colonel Fauntleroy,
Major R. A. Ogden, and an officer of the Engineer Corps,
were appointed as a committee to select a site on the
Smoky Hill River for a ten-company calvary post. The
point chosen was the present site of Fort Riley. Fort
Riley was started in 1853, to protect the Indians against
the aggression of the white settlers who were coming in.
At this time Kansas was still a part of the unorganised
territory.

On May 19, 1855, Captain Lovell, of the Sixth Infantry formed an encampment at the mouth of the Pawnee

1. Andreas, Op. Cit., p. 1300.
2. Ibid.

River and named it "Camp Center." July 26, 1853, it took
the name of Fort Riley.[1] The building of the post was
under the supervision of Major Ogden. Major Ogden remained in charge of the post until his death in 1855
when cholera swept Fort Riley. In 1854, there were four
companies, sixteen officers and 228 men,[2] with an unknown
number of laborers located at Fort Riley. These men were
under martial law and were allowed no part in civil
government, so they had little influence in determing the
development of Riley County.

The northern part of the county was not settled in
the early days of Riley County. It was settled up as far
as Keats and later to Randolph. In the latter part of
1853, a Tennessean, Samuel P. Dyer, was running a government ferry at Juniata, about one mile below Rocky Ford.
Shortly afterwards a government bridge was put in at this
point, but it was destroyed by flood waters in the winter
of 1855.[3] Mr. Dyer is one of the first white[4] settlers of
Riley County and this interesting description is given of
him. "He died in February, 1873. His politics were Pro-

1. Andreas, Wm. Hist., p. 1300.
2. Ibid., p. ...
3. Ibid., p. 1301.
4. Authorities do not agree on this point. The
   Secretary's Book of the Manhattan Town Association
   states that Colonel Parks was the first white
   settler, however they may mean of Manhattan Town
   Site.

slavery. He was of good, common sense, excellent judgment and great kindness of heart. His home was one story
high and two stories long." [1]

The first home missionary of Riley County was the
Reverend Charles Emerson Blood, a native of Mason, New
Hampshire, who located at Juniata, November 4, 1854.
"Moving with others in his own words,'left their homes in
the States, not simply to improve their worldly interests,
but to fight the battle of freedom and save this beautiful country from the blighting curse of slavery.' " [2]

In 1855 Zeandale Township was named by J. H. Pillsbury. Zeandale was named to mean "corn-dale." In 1855 a
church edifice was begun but never completed, and on
alternate Sundays, during the year 1858, the Reverend
Harvey Jones of Wabaunsee preached here. The first
school was established and taught by Mrs. Pillsbury in
her home. In 1858, Miss Mattie Keys established a
private school and in 1860, Miss Keys became the teacher
of the first district school, held on the farm of Mr.
Abner Allen. [3] The first school house was built in 1863.
It was made of hewn logs and called the "Conic Section"

1. Andreas, Op. cit., p. 1301.
2. Ibid.
3. Ibid.

because of its hexagonal shape.

The next township to be established was Ashland, then a part of Davis County. It was transferred to Riley County by an act of the legislature in 1873. Ashland was first settled by Thomas Reynolds in 1855. On April 23, 1855 a colony made up in Covington, Kentucky and Cincinnati, Ohio, arrived, consisting of thirty-five members. These settlers came by steamer from Cincinnati to Kansas City, and from there in immigrant wagons.[1] Among these people were many admirers of Henry Clay and the name of his late residence was given to this township. "The settlement was made on Mc Dowell Creek. F. G. Adams was president, the Reverend H. B. White, Vice President, and Henry J. Adams treasure. Ashland was the county seat of Davis County and several terms of the district court were held there. A post office was established in 1858.[2] Dr. K. L. Pateo was the first court clerk and he became county treasurer of Riley County in 1860.

Ogden Township, was named for Major Ogden of the United States Army. In June of 1854, Thomas Reynolds erected the first dwelling and here was held the election

1. Andreas, Op. Cit., p. 1301.
2. Ibid.

for the first territorial delegate, November 24, of 1854.[1]

In 1855 the first store in the township was opened at Pawnee by Robert Wilson. Shortly afterward a Mr. Johnson of Kansas City opened the first store in Ogden. The first saw and corn mill was brought in in 1856 by J. W. Parsons. Theodore Weichselbaum "its most prominent merchant" came to Ogden in 1860, and for years did a large freighting business across the plains. He had a chain of five stores in western forts. Thomas Dixon built a large ware house north of where the railroad track now is and did an extensive shipping business. There was also a blacksmith, a shoemaker, a carpenter, a wagon-maker, a saddler, a general mechanic, and an auctioneer. The first school was opened in 1859 and by 1865 there were two churches, a Congregational and a Roman Catholic Church. The property value of the latter was $ 1,200.[2]

The Ogden town company was chartered by the legislature of 1857 and a town at once laid out in blocks and lots. A hotel, the Union Pacific House, was built immediately. In the April 11, 1857, issue of the Kansas

---

1. Andreas, Op Cit., p. 1301.
2. Andreas, History of State of Kansas, p. 1301.

Weekly Herald there is a statement noting the location of
the land office for the western district of Kansas at
Ogden. It gave the location of Ogden as "four and a half
miles from Fort Riley on roads leading to western posts.
Its proximity to the government post and good situation
upon principal roads, give it advantages which few towns
possess. The location of the land office will form another great source of prosperity, and Ogden is, no doubt,
destined to become a point of importance. Shares in the
town are now sold at $ 300.00" [1]

Another interesting notice appears in the October
3d, 1857, issue of the Kansas Weekly Herald. "Ogden the
county seat of Riley County is a new town. Scarcely a
year old, with 200 inhabitants, also headquarters of the
western land district and the county seat of justice.
Two hotels are underway and improvements of substantial
character going on. It is a fine place for the location
of business men and mechanics. I consider the prospects
of Ogden as decidedly among the best in the upper portion
of the Kaw valley......Manhattan, one of the Boston and
Cincinnatti towns was gotten up for speculation. I think

---

1. The Kansas Weekly Herald, April, 11, 1857.

years will develop the superior natural location of
Ogden." 1

Bala Township was named after a town in North Wales.
In the spring of 1868, Mr. A. L. Phelps settled on the
fork of Timber Creek, near the present site of Bala,
though the Welsh colony which finally settled Bala was
not organized until 1870, in New York.

Jackson Township was settled in 1855 by Gardner
Randolph and his family. In 1856 Edward and Soloman
Secrest and Henry Shellenbaum, all natives of Switzerland,
settled there. Randolph, first called Waterville, was
laid out in 1856 by J. K. Whitson, however its real
development did not begin until the early seventies.

Grant Township was settled in 1855 by S. D. Huston
and Henry Babcock. It was named after President Grant.

Stockdale is noted for one thing, the fact that in
a very early day they had a sawmill. The various town-
ships which are mentioned here, with the exception of
Manhattan, which will be treated separately, were settled
after 1870, so they have not been discussed.

Western Kansas (then Riley County and surrounding
country) was early known as "The Great American Desert."

---

1. The Kansas Weekly Herald, April, 24, 1857.

Yet even Napoleon recognized this as being false.[1] The
Express stated that it was started by Missouri. "The
composition of its soil is so varied in its chemical
elements that almost everything in the nature of grasses,
grains, fruits, and vegetables can be produced from it.
The dark, easily worked soil of the bottom lands is very
productive."[2]

In 1857, Governor Geary went on a tour of inspection
through Kansas, as then settled. Mention was made of
Manhattan and Fort Riley. "At this point the party
turned toward Fort Riley, the western limits of the route.
Encamping at Centropolis, at the head waters of the
Wakarusa and the Neosho River, they crossed the Kansas
River on the 1n of October, at Riley City,[3] then con-
taining eight houses, and arrived the same evening at Fort
Riley, where they remained until the 31, the visit being
enlivened by a ball and review of the troops."[4] On his
return trip to Lecompton, Governor Geary encamped Sunday,
November 2, on the south bank of the Kansas River opposite
Manhattan. The citizens of that town had assembled to
hear preaching by the Reverend Charles E. Blood, who, on

1. Manhattan Express, March 28, 1860.
2. Andreas, Op. Cit., p. 1300.
3. Riley City as mentioned here, is extinct and it has
      been impossible to find where it was located.
4. Andreas, Op. Cit., p. 156

learning that the governor was in the neighborhood, adjourned the meeting, and crossing the river with several other men in a small boat, visited his camp, and prevailed upon him to speak to the congregation on the exciting topics of the day.[1] Manhattan is described as "located in a valley of great fertility, and containing about one hundred and fifty inhabitants, generally moral, intelligent and industrious, who took no part in the recent disturbances." [2] It contained a steam saw and grist mill, three stores and a hotel.

During the territorial days of Kansas, steamboats came up the river to Manhattan and as far as Junction City. The Big Blue, which formed a large portion of the eastern boundary of Riley County had fewer sharp bends than the Kaw into which it flowed east of Manhattan. It furnished so much water power it was called the "Merrimac of Kansas." It was dammed at Rocky Ford some three miles above Manhattan so that there was a fall of ten feet, the dam being 368 feet in length. The dam was all built of heavy oak timber bolted into the solid rock foundations.[3] The Rocky Ford Mill was built in 1868. A four story

1. Andreas, Op. Cit., p. 155.
2. Ibid.
3. Ibid., p. 1301.

store building, forty feet by sixty feet, "There are
quite a variety of kinds of timber of which the most
abundant are cottonwood, several kinds of oak and elm,
black walnut, soft maple, hackberry, hickory, locust, ash,
linden, sycamore, mulberry, box alder, and coffee-bean.
Of the cultivated groves soft maple predominated, though
black walnut, locust and cotton wood are quite common."[1]
There were large walnut groves around Keats which furnished a great deal of lumber for the houses in Manhattan.
Since Walnut was the common material it was used by the
people for the frames and substantial part of their homes
and if they could not afford otherwise it was used
throughout. However those who could afford it usually
went to Leavenworth and got white pine for finishing the
inside and for the woodwork.

In 1855 cholera swept Fort Riley and Major Ogden
and Major Wood's wife and four children, their servant
girl and her husband died. Due to this plague the troops,
Dr. Simons, the army physician, and the ladies fled the
post and created a great deal of excitement in Riley
County. Deaths occurred at the rate of twelve to thirteen
per day. By September, the health of the Post and of

1. Andreas, Op. Cit., p. 1301.

Riley County was finally restored and the public work
continued. A monument of native stone was erected to
Major Ogden and placed on the highest point so that it
might overlook the Fort and every one could see it.[1]

In February of 1860 there was talk of changing the
county seat of Riley County to Manhattan and it was form-
ally decided by ballot. There was a great deal of oppo-
sition because of the expense involved in erecting a new
building and changing offices and the people, who had met
in a large group at the Manhattan city hall, decided to
petition the legislature so the bill would not be introduced.[2] However the county seat was changed because in
the issue of the Manhattan Express for July 7, 1860 there
appeared an editorial on Riley County taxes. It stated
that the taxes were too high and that there was fraud
involved on the part of two citizens who represented
Riley County. At that time they attempted to move the
county seat back to Ogden and reduce the taxes.

In the latter part of 1860 the total indebtedness
of Riley County was seventy dollars. In the next few
years there was to be a decided increase and change in
the economic status, brought on by the drought, crop

1. Kansas Territorial Register, September 19, 1865.
2. Manhattan Express, February 1, 1860.

failures, speculation, and the War. Also a decided
growth in population and wealth of the people.

CHAPTER III---GENERAL SURVEY OF MANHATTAN UP TO 1867

"We the undersigned to wit; E. M. Thurston, S. D.
Huston, E. A. Wilcoxe, I. T. Goodnow, C. H. Lovejoy, C. F.
Blood, M. E. Wright, C. M. Wilson, T. J. Roosa, A.
Morrison, H. P. Frisby, C. Godard Jr., R. R. Crane, F.
Flagg, A. L. Prentice, J. Hoar, Simeon Perry, G. W.
Lockwood, E. B. Gage, J. K. Bissell, Cyrus Bishop, A.
Browning, D. Ambrose and N. B. Neeley, associate our-
selves together for the purpose of occupying and improv-
ing for a town site, ten quarter sections of land (more
or less) in Kansas Territory, situated at the junction of
the Big Blue and Kansas Rivers and agreed to by the
following constitution.

Article I.

This organization shall be known by the name of the
Boston Association of Kansas Territory." 1

Those settlers met at the junction of the Big Blue
and Kansas, April 3, 1855 for consultation in reference
to a town site. A committee was appointed to examine the

1. Constitution of the Boston Town Association, Secre-
      tary's Book of Manhattan Town Association.

ground and to report the amount of land desirable for a
town site. The same evening at seven o'clock, in Mr.
Wrights tent a meeting was held to hear the report of the
committee and determine the town site. At this time
Manhattan was a village of tents, though even then a
very lawful and orderly village as contrasted to most
pioneer settlements.

The first annual report of the trustees to the stockholders of the Manhattan Town Association gave briefly
the history of Manhattan up to the date of the report,
January 7, 1856.

A portion of the town site, as maped out by the
Boston Town Association, was first settled in 1854, by
G. S. Park. In November of the same year Mr. Park erected a cabin which was the first building raised on what is
at the present time Manhattan. The name chosen by Mr.
Park was Poleska, a Greek word meaning central city. Mr.
Park spent the following winter in Texas and did not return to Poleska until April of 1855.[1] Andreas in his
History of Kansas says that Seth L. Childs built the
first house, but since his book was not published until
1883, I will use the other source.

_____

1. Secretary's Book of Manhattan Town Association,
   1855 to 1856.

In the mean time a company had been organized by Mr.
Wilcoxe, Russell and others, to commence operations at
the mouth of the Big Blue River. This however did not
include the quarter section on which Mr. Park had built
his cabin. This new place was named Canton.[1]

The last of March 1855, Messers, Lovejoy, Goodnow,
Wilson, and others came to this place and commenced on
the ground previously settled by Mr. Park and the Canton
Company.

On March 24, 1855, Isaac T. Goodnow, Luke F. Lincoln,
C. H. Lovejoy, C. N. Wilson, Joseph Winterscaid, and N. R.
Wright, a committee of a New England Company which left
Boston on March 6, 1855, one week ahead of a company of
some two hundred who left March 13, 1855 and eventually
settled in Canton."[2] These men went to St. Louis on the
railroad, then up the Missouri River, which took eight
days. At Kansas City oxen, horses and wagons were secured. Five days after leaving Kansas City they reached
Juniata, five mile above where Manhattan is now located.

Juniata was a "pro-slavery" town located close to
the government bridge which had been built at a cost of

1. Secretary's Book of Manhattan Town Association,
   1855 to 1859.
2. Isaac T. Goodnow, Personal Reminiscences and Kansas
   1855, Kansas Historical Collection, Vol. VI, (1855-
   1859) p. 245.

ten thousand dollars. The principal settler was an old
"six foot" Virginian,[1] by the name of Dyer, and a member
of the M. E. Church South. "His cabin, as described by
an exploring missionary, was one story high and three
stories long. His wife excused him to the same missionary for not saying grace at the table by saying, 'My old
man, since coming to the new country, has lost his
manners.' " These people kept a sort of free hotel and
store. It was a preaching place for all denominations
and it was customary after sermon to invite everybody to
dinner. "They were a noble, generous-hearted old couple,
but their free table and dishonest clerk soon got away
with most of their property." [2]

The destruction of the bridge, the following winter,
and the changing government road, with the rivalry of
Manhattan which followed, effectually wiped out the town.
In Kansas a "pro-slavery" town could not live by the side
of a free state town.

Here Goodnow and his friends, met the Reverend
Charles E. Blood, a missionary of the Congregational
Church. After looking over the surrounding country the

---

1. Goodnow, Op. Cit., p. 245.
2. Ibid.

committee decided to locate here. They soon learned of
Park's settlement and after careful deliberation, March
26, 1855, Goodnow pitched his tent on the Park town site
about thirty rods from his blacksmith shop.[1] There was
some difficulty over the claim, as a man named Martin
claimed it. Goodnow in his paper, Personal Reminiscences
and Kansas Emigration 1855, said this was the only dispute
of the kind he knew of to be settled without a fight. "To
save the town site from jumpers, several shake houses
were built and placed on each quarter section with some
one to occupy and hold it as a claim till it could be
preempted with a 'float.' "[2] Not half of the original
company ever reached Manhattan. Some stopped by the way,
some became discouraged by hardships, and of those who
reached there about one half left at the end of the first
season.[3]

On reaching Canton the two companies effected a
consolidation and named the town Boston.[4] The improvements at that time consisted of a log cabin, built by
Colonel Park for a blacksmith shop, and a dug-out at the
foot of Blue Mont. On March 30, 1855, Mr. A. D. Boston

---

1. Goodnow, Op. Cit., p. 248.
2. Ibid., p. 248-249, (a float is an Indian land warrant
   for 640 acres of land and was transferable by
   purchase.)
3. Ibid., p. 250.
4. Andreas, History of the State of Kansas, p. 1300.

was elected representative from this district to the first
territorial legislature." [1]

On April 4, 1855, a consolidation of all these town
interests was effected. Twenty-four persons were present
at the meeting and these organized as the Boston Association and officially named the town Boston. One of the
houses erected was used by Goodnow as a store, the first
store to be located here.

On April 27, 1855, a colony left Cincinnati for
central Kansas, by way of the Ohio, Mississippi, Missouri
and Kansas Rivers. The name of Manhattan had been fixed
upon as that of the prospective town. This name was
chosen because they thought there would be room for a
town that might bear some comparison to New York City.[2]
At St. Louis this company numbered about eighty people.
Deeming the steamer Hartford, which had the Cincinnati
and Kansas Land Company on board,[3] an abolition boat, the
authorities at St. Louis, delayed her for some days. A
pilot was hired at the extravagant price of $ 7.50[4] and
the voyage from St. Louis was begun. Cholera broke out

1. Andreas, Cir. Cit., p. 1800.
2. Ibid., p. 1300.
3. Secretary's Book of Manhattan Town Association.
4. Andreas, p. 1306.

and several members died. Arriving at Kansas City, there
was a tarry of a week because of low water on the Kansas
River, and, when, at Lecompton, the steamer got a ground,
another heavy rain so raised the river that there was no
further delay until the steamer passed the mouth of the
Big Blue on June 1, 1855. About a mile and a half above
the mouth of the Blue the steamer grounded and was obliged to land its passengers and freight. At this time the
company numbered seventy-five persons. They had brought
with them ten frame houses already to put up.[1]

John Pipher, Andrew J. Mead, and E. Palmer hired
wagons and drove to what is now Junction City and there
laid out the town of Manhattan. During their absence
there was an interview with the Boston Association, which
resulted in the Boston Association voting to give half
the town site to the Cincinnati Company if they would
settle there and help build up the town.[2] The contract
was agreed upon and after this last marriage the name of
the town was changed to Manhattan, in order that the
Cincinnati Company might fulfil the agreement in the
constitution they had made with their backers, one of

1. James A. Humphrey, The Country West of Topeka Prior
      to 1865, Kansas State Historical Collection, Vol.
      IV (1886-1888), p. 291.
2. Andreas, Op. Cit., p. 1300.

these agreements being that the town they settle be
named Manhattan.

The land on which Manhattan was built had at one
time been an Indian float and it was necessary for the
settlers to buy up this land before building or locating.

Andreas in his History of Kansas gives this description of Manhattan. "Manhattan township embraces about
forty square miles. On this territory is the beautiful
city of Manhattan, watered by the Big Blue and the
Kansas Rivers, and Wild Cat Creek. Its bottom lands are
very extensive. South of the Kansas River, Mount Pro-
spect rises almost to a perpendicular height of more than
800 feet above the river and Blue Mont nearly as high." [1]
At this time it was necessary to ascend Blue Mont from
the north, the south side was considered as impassable.
"Although the town drew to its bosom a varied population,
its leading characteristics were of the New England type.
While its material progress was carefully attended to
and watched with solicitude and interest, it early became
the scene of much mental activity. In 1866 a literary
society was incorporated and organized, a circulating
library collected, and weekly meetings for discussion

1. Andreas, Op. Cit., p. 1306.

and other literary exercises were conducted under its
auspices." 1

Besides this an association was formed and incorporated for the establishment of a college. A site of one
hundred acres was secured west of town and title procured. Professor Isaac T. Goodnow spent several years in
the east getting funds for buildings, library, apparatus
and furnishings. Sale of Manhattan town lots was set
aside for this and in 1859, "the walls of the Bluemont
College buildings began to rise. The corner stone was
laid with elaborate ceremony May 10, 1859, with speeches
from General Pomeroy and others. It was opened to
students about a year later. In 1863 it was turned over,
with a library of 2,000 volumes, its apparatus and land,
as a gift to the state for a State Agricultural College.
September 2, 1863, the Agricultural College opened, with
the Reverend Joseph Denison, president." 2

During the early years, population did not increase
rapidly in this part of Kansas. The means of transportation were meager and expensive, but it expanded and
pushed slowly westward. "Ogden caught the debris of

1. Goodnow, Op. Cit., Vol. IV, pp. 291 and 292.
2. Ibid., p. 292.

Faunce when that ill-fated town was swept from its moor-
ing by an official cyclone from Washington." It became
the county seat of Riley County and retained it until
1858 when it was removed to Manhattan. The commercial
idea was the chief incentive to the founding of Manhattan. Here "the original scheme comprehended a finished
community; schools, churches, college, libraries and
literary societies all existed in embryo, ready to be
launched forth at the earliest opportunity. Here the
social, intellectual and moral needs of the people were
anticipated."[1]

Manhattan, being near the fort and in the midst of a
large farming country, the productiveness of the soil for
years repaid in a large measure all labor bestowed upon
it. Formerly all supplies for the fort had been brought
one hundred and fifty miles, or from Missouri, so there
was a ready market for all local produce. The fact that
Manhattan was surrounded by two large rivers and many
streams made it compare favorably with any territory and
assured plenty of good farming land, plenty of timber
and a means of transportation to connect it with Kansas
City and St. Louis.

---

1. Goodnow, Op. Cit., Vol. IV, p. 394.

In April of 1860, the editor of the Topeka Tribune
visited Manhattan and on his return published an article
describing Manhattan as a city beautifully situated "at
the junction of the Kaw and Blue Rivers, on a beautiful
plain; just level enough to make it one of the most
beautiful town sites in Kansas."[1] At that time two
churches were already completed and another one was being constructed. The Bluemont College had been established and in spite of the drought, they predicted that Manhattan would obtain a place of considerable importance.

On February 14, 1859, the legislature of Kansas
passed the Act of Incorporation for the city of Manhattan
and on Monday, January 2, 1860, it was taken before the
trustees[2] of the Manhattan Town Association to be acted
upon. A request was made to stockholders, asking that
all be present or appoint some one with the power of
attorney to act for them. At this time the people appeared to be intensely interested in their local government. Shares were purchased in the Town Association and
stockholders played a very important part. From time to
time notices appear in the papers, notifying stockholders

1. Topeka Tribune, April 14, 1860.
2. Manhattan Express, December 24, 1859.

of meetings and calling public meetings at the city hall
or court house.

In June 16, 1860, The Manhattan Town Association
granted the final deed to all holders of certificates of
shares and bonds to perfect the title to city property.[1]
On June 30, 1860, the first census was taken in Kansas
Territory.[2] In the year 1860, a number of improvements
were made in the city. Mr. Woodman, built a beautiful
two story residence twenty feet by twenty-eight feet.
Mr. Currie completed a similar residence near the college.
Mr. John Mails erected a new store building on Poynts.
Mr. Harper built a new residence and the new Methodist
Episcopal Church, described as the most beautiful beyond
St. Louis, was completed. The spire of the church tower-
ed seventy-five feet above ground. In the winter of 1859
the grading and macadamising of Poynts was begun. A rock
crushing machine was procured and the work was completed
in the spring of 1860. This was the first street of its
kind west of Topeka.[3]

In May 1f 1861, W. H. Smythe, of Manhattan, introduced a bill in the Kansas legislature, to cut off from

1. Manhattan Express, June 16, 1860.
2. _____, 1860.
3. Manhattan Express, December 24, 1859.

the city of Manhattan all portions lying outside of the
Wyandotte floats and restrict the city limits to twelve
hundred and forty acres. The citizens of Manhattan opposed this, saying it revoked a portion of their rights,
entirely without their consent.[1]

"Our Town," an article published in the Manhattan
Express December 24, 1859, describes Manhattan as the
most westerly city east of the Rocky Mountains. "The
majority of all the inhabitants are people who have become civilized and believing, 'that in union is strength,'
have built houses tolerably close together and live in
them when at home. The Sabbath having been from time
immemorial, regarded as a day of rest, it is a duty which
they consider they owe to society to respect it and in
conforming with the example have erected several elegant
church edifices of solid stone where they all assemble
once a week. We have a school house of no one-horse
dimensions, Societies, bevolent, literary and sportive.

Our prospects are flattering and, we hope in no
distant day to become permanent things. Stone and timber
abound in abundance. Access to the river is free and
easy. The climate is sufficiently changeable to satisfy

1. Manhattan Express, December 24, 1859.

everyone.

The town is located upon what was two Wyandotte floats. One hundred ten miles from the Missouri River and sixteen miles from Fort Riley. "Sunset sublimely glorious and moonshine gloriously sublime."

As to comforts and amusements we defy competition. We have all kinds of vegetables and fruits common in civilized communities of the north, such as corn, beans, potatoes, turnips, of the fleshy, beef, pork, venison, turkey, buffalo-meat, rabbits, squirrel, chickens, of the fish, salmon, eat, pike, shad and gars."[1]

This last sketch gives a fairly good description of Manhattan. During the war it continued much as it had in the past. Manhattan raised its quota of troops, had a home guard, and its heroes. One of these was Nehemiah Green who after the war returned to Kansas and became one of its governors. There was a gradual increase in wealth and population and the intellectual interest of the people. Manhattan became an educational center of Kansas and one of which the people were very proud. As early as 1859 there was talk of a railroad and in 1860 the government began the road from Leavenworth to Denver

---

1. *Manhattan Express*, December 24, 1859.

or the Pikes Peak road.

CHAPTER IV---ECONOMIC DEVELOPMENT

Agriculture

The chief concern of pioneers is the economic development of their country and the people of Riley county were no exception. The first crop was planted here in 1854 by Dyer, at Juniata. He raised enough food stuffs for his own needs, but did not attempt to produce more than a small amount. The first real cultivation was begun in the spring of 1855 and the colony advanced successfully and rapidly until the summer of 1859 and 1860 when a drought set in which ruined all the crops and left the people practically without means of existence. It was during this period that the eastern states sent their money and food to Kansas. Kansas Aid and Relief Societies were formed through out the east, especially the north east, and Pomeroy was able to use the needs of Kansas as a means of increasing his own wealth and fame.

Manhattan had every advantage necessary to the success of an agricultural community "Being near the fort, and in the midst of a rich farming country, the productivity of the soil for years must repay in a large measure all labor bestowed upon it.

A friend, who located not many miles from Manhattan in the spring, and cultivated a few acres, in the fall found himself the possessor of $ 7,000 more than when he came. He sold at the fort whatever he raised, at large prices.[1] All supplies from the fort at that time were brought from Missouri, which was nearly one hundred and fifty miles from the fort. It was no wonder the fort provided a ready market for Manhattan and vicinity.

The first corn crop was planted June 19, 1855 and sold at home for Fort Riley market at $ 1.25 per bushell. Eggs sold at 62½ cents per dozen. Pumpkins were ripe by the fourth of July and were described by the settlers as the largest ever seen. The blue stem, prairie grass was so high, they could tie it over their heads while sitting on their horses.[2]

At first supplies came from the river one hundred twenty miles away. It took two weeks with horses or oxen to make this journey.

The first winter some of the settlers dried corn in the oven and ground it in coffee mills. This corn meal,

1. Sara T. L. Robinson, Kansas, The Interior and Exterior Life, Boston; Crosby, Nichols and Co., 1855, p. 186.
2. Goodnow, Op. Cit., Vol. IV, p. 280.

it was said, "made the best kind of bread." [1] The
arrival of the emigrant aid mill from Lawrence, drawn by
twenty yoke of oxen, was a great event. It simplified
milling and though more expensive gave the farmers time
they needed for other things.

Wild turkey, prarie chicken, quail, rabbits, coons,
possum, wild deer, wild cats and wolves, furnished a
great variety of game. Meat could be salted down and
preserved for the winter and most of the game mentioned
was plentiful. To obtain buffalo meat it was usually
necessary to travel about a hundred miles out on the
plains. Hunting parties were organized for the trips
and usually a month passed before they returned.
Business was very good as long as they kept clear of the
war-like Cheyennes. [2]

Fruit growing was greatly encouraged "This is a
fruit country, nearly all farmers may raise their own
fruit. Strawberries, rasberries, currants, and goose-
berries grow or will grow almost anywhere. They can be
canned or preserved the whole year. Apples, pears,
peaches and cherries can be raised on most farms. There
is no good reason why fruit should not be as plentiful

1. Goodnow, Op. Cit., Vol. IV, p. 250.
2. Ibid.

as corn or wheat.

"This is a billious country, that is people who live here are especially liable to billious diseases. There is perhaps, no other preventative of billious diseases than the constant use of fruits as a part of the diet. It corrects the acids and juices of the stomach and assists digestion. It keeps the bowls properly active, prevents sluggishness and torpidity which promote billious derangements. Fruit, to do its best office in the diet should be cooked and eaten as a part of the regular meal. Thus used, how delicious it is......There-fore let us grow it on all our farms, and adorn and make pleasant all our tables." [1]

The first peaches of Riley County were raised by C. E. Bleed on his farm near the College site in the summer of 1860.[2] Mr. Bleed had the best and one of the few orchards in Riley County though people were becoming more interested. Due to a number of failures in the few pre-ceding years people thought they could not raise fruit here and would have to depend on Missouri. This was probably due to the handling and shipping of the trees

1. Western Kansas Express, August 20, 1860.
2. Ibid., September, 20, 1860.

and bushes. Reverend Blood proved that fruit could be raised here. He had about forty peach trees, twenty-six of which were bearing in 1861, also a number of apple and cherry trees. The interest in fruit raising gradually increased until almost every home had its own fruit supply and own orchar. Choice three year old apple trees were advertised at $ 13.00 per 100 or $ 12.00 per 100 by the 1,000. [1]

This interest culminated in establishing the Union Agricultural Society, which was able by 1368 to hold its own fruit show. Sixteen varieties of apples were displayed and discussed and five varieties of peaches. [2]

Wheat was gradually being recognized as the best and most suitable crop for Kansas. In 1859 there was a great wheat crop everywhere. Cotton, hay, corn, and sugar gave greater yield than ever before. The wheat crop was estimated at two hundred million bushells, against 150,500,-000 bushel in 1858, 180,000,000 bushel in 1859, and 100,-000,000 bushel in 1850. In 1859 wheat was selling:

In Cincinnati for $ 1.10 a bushel for prime red
    "   "   "   " $ 1.16 "   "   "   "   white

1. Manhattan Express, June 8, 1860.
2. Manhattan Standard, September 19, 1868.

In New York   for $ 1.30- $1.36 a bushel for prime red.

In New York   for $ 1.55- $1.66 "   "   "   " white.

In Philadelphia for $ 1.20- $1.30 a bushel for prime red.

In Philadelphia for $ 135 a bushell for prime white.[1]

The first of September was regarded as the proper time to prepare wheat land and sow the wheat. It was to be put in with harrow, cultivator or double shared plow. One bushel and a peck per acre was considered the proper amount. The people were advised to sow largely, but not more than they could care for well. In 1859 "Tom Linn" picked up 3,800 bushel of corn at Manhattan and took it by steamer to Kansas City.[2]

August was described as the "idle month," an ideal time to plow wheat or oat stubbles, in order to cultivate corn and potatoes next season. By doing this they might enrich the land and prevent weeds, also expose the plowed land to the suns rays, destroy insects and save labor the next spring. It was a good time to erect sheds for prarie hay and straw and make any repairs that were needed.[3]

The prospects for a wheat crop in 1860 were very

1. Western Kansas Express, August 20, 1859.
2. George W. Martin, The Territorial and Military Com- bine at Fort Riley, Vol. VII of Collections of the Kansas State Historical Society.
3. Western Kansas Express, August 20, 1859.

good. In June there was plenty of rain, the crops looked exceedingly good and the farmers were in high spirits.
In July, though there was some rain there was fear of
drought. This article appeared in the Manhattan Express
for July 14, 1860. "Friday another sprinkle, though
still fear of drought. Corn, the great western staple
may not get enough rain and this crop is important.
Much depends on it. A failure will greatly affect the
young herds of stock in process of development in
Kansas." 1

As late as July 20, there was a slight rain, though
only enough to settle the dust. There was hope, that
some late fields of corn, if furnished with plenty of
rain that week, might yield a half a crop. The earliest
corn was too far gone to make anything but fodder. The
tassels had been killed by extreme heat and drought.

George W. Martin in his paper The Territorial and
Military Combine at Fort Riley says that "the drought of
1860 began September 1, 1860, from which date there was
no rain until September or October 1860,.....There were
no resources whatever, and doubtless aid was needed, but
its abuse, political and otherwise, reflected on Kansas

----

1. Manhattan Express, July 14.

for a decade. A committee of the legislature stated
that there were 30,000 people dependent for subsistence
upon outside sources. On the 13 of July the mercury
went up to 112 and 114 in the shade, and a hot scorching
wind kept it at these figures for weeks. The dates of
the beginning and ending of the drought vary in locations
but it may be said in general that they were from twelve
to fourteen months." [1]

The relief committee of Kansas organised in 1860,
had up to January 1, 1861, distributed throughout the
territory, 1,052,582 pounds of provisions and seed, and
between January 1, and March 16, 1861, 7,099,330 pounds.
Also $ 83,889,82 in money. This did not include cloth-
ing, medecine, and garden seed. Members of the committee were sent as agents to various eastern cities to
collect the supplies and funds. J. S. Pomeroy was in
charge of the Kansas Relief fund. [2]

On December 1, 1860 [3] Riley County had turned down
all aid offered. They said that it was not needed here
and should be used in districts more seriously affected.
On December 28, 1860, [4] word had been received by the

1. George W. Martin, Op. Cit., pp. 25 and 26.
2. Ibid., p. 26.
3. Western Kansas Express, December 1, 1860.
4. Ibid., December 28, 1860.

Riley County relief committee that they were to receive a large supply of provisions for distribution among the suffering of the county. In the meantime the Kansas Relief Bill had passed both Houses of the National Congress. [1]

An agent of the New England Kansas Relief Committee was in Manhattan, January 22. [2] Delegates of Riley County and many counties around met in Manhattan City Hall, January 12, to ascertain the real condition of the poor and suffering in western Kansas and reports were made from various localities. A Massachusetts Kansas Relief Committee was organized to distribute food, clothing and money. The sum of $ 12,400 was received from this committee. [3]

One of the dispatches of Thaddeus Hyatt in describing conditions in Kansas greatly exaggerates them. It reads, "starvation in Kansas, frightful prospects. But one step between 15,000 people and death. An appeal to the Press of the country, to the churches, to Congress to state legislatures, to philanthropists, to the human everywhere." This caused a great deal of trouble and in

1. Western Kansas Express, December 1, 1860.
2. Ibid., January 28, 1861.
3. Ibid., February 25, 1860.

the editorial of the Western Kansas Express, March 23,
1861, Hyatt and Pomeroy are severly attacked for the
picture given. The editor said, that some relief was
needed but that Hyatt made conditions more serious than
they were and too highly colored. Up to the last year
Kansas crops had been abundant, and proved the fertility
and productiveness of Kansas and the drought was not
confined to Kansas alone. The farmers here were men of
comparatively small capital and as most of the surplus
had been invested in farm-improvements their last years,
crop failure found them unprepared for the emergency.

In March, 1861, Dr. A. Hunting received clothing
from friends in Providence Rhode Island. This was
valued at $ 300.00 by Lewis Kurtz, a local merchant, and
contained shoes, hosiery, boots, caps, and other articles
of clothing. Most of this was distributed in Manhattan,
but a part of the supplies were sent to relieve other
counties.[1] In April of 1861, Mr. A. Y. Mead of Manhattan received one of the last relief consignments. This
consignment consisted of potatoes for free distribution
among farmers of Riley County for planting.

Mr. Hyatt and Mr. Pomeroy were justly accused of

---

1. Western Kansas Express, March 16, 1861.

profiting from the Kansas drought and increasing their wealth. After this headway and progress in Kansas was very slow and in 1874 a second great drought hit Kansas.[1]

In September of 1860, they began to sow their next years crop. The weather was favorable. The success of the crop depended partly on the manner in which it was put in the ground. Farmers were advised to have the ground already plowed. Then to use a drill to plant it, because it required less seed, bury it two and one half inches deep and use a heavy roller to cover it so it would hold the moisture.

In April of 1861, heavy rains gave the farmer renewed hope of a crop. Vegetation was beginning to come to life and the fall wheat looked most promising. Farmers were planting a large crop and hoped to be able to recover from last years drought. The weather continued favorable during April, but owing to the last years failure and the inexperience of the people with the climate there was a general feeling of distrust. The wheat crop for the year was successful. And though the August weather was hot and oppressive an abundant hay crop was harvested.

---

1. George W. Martin, Op. Cit., p. 28.

In May, 1862, the crop future was very bright. The wheat had never looked better and there was already enough rain to mature the crop. Farmers were busily engaged in planting their late crops.[1] There was some talk of locusts, but they were not to be found in any number. They had made their appearance in some parts of the country and there was a feeling that they would appear every twenty years. In the Manhattan Express for June 21, 1862 appeared this article, "crop prospects still good. Wheat is doing exceedingly well. Only danger apprehended is from the locusts."

By 1862, wheat was becoming more and more the chief crop. Greater attention was given it. Most newspapers and magazines were carrying instructions in regard to raising it and the adaptibility of western Kansas to raising it. Spring wheat was contrasted to winter wheat and all phases of it were discussed and studied.

Hay was another very important crop and the crops of 1861, 1862, and 1863, had been increasing in size and of excellent quality. Farmers were advised to make the most of it. As late as 1863, potatoes were looked upon as an uncertain crop in Kansas. The soil was con-

---

1. Manhattan Express, May 17, 1862.

sidered good, but the climate was regarded as unsuitable.
Mr. A. B. Whitford began an experiment in this field.
He had the ground plowed, a drill dropped the seed in
furrows, it was covered with a plow then leveled off and
the whole surface covered with straw four inches deep.
By this method he was able to raise nearly 200 bushel an
acre.

The war did not greatly affect the economic development of Riley County or of Kansas. No actual fight-
ing occurred here and they were able to supply their
quota of troops. Prices were higher, but even their
advancement was very gradual and continued much as it
had in the years already discussed. Marketing was still
a problem, since with the increased production Fort
Riley could not take care of all the produce. In 1863,
nine wagon loads of wheat left Manhattan for Denver in
hope of securing a better market. In September of the
same year a Missourian passed through Manhattan with a
wagon load of apples. He was asking three dollars a
bushel.

It was in this year that sweet potatoes were first
cultivated, by the Reverend R. D. Parker.[1] Many new

1. Manhattan Standard, September 19, 1863.

foods were introduced and grown successfully. Kansas was coming into her own agriculturally through a slow and steady growth, not sensational, but nevertheless very successful.

business

The people who settled Manhattan displayed an early interest in its commercial development. In the report of the Secretary of the Manhattan Town Association for August 21, 1856 it was voted that one, Mr. Tallison be invited to establish a press and weekly paper at this place, and if he complied, he was to be considered an original member of the Manhattan Town Association without paying back assessments. There seems to have been a premium on original membership. They also voted to grant the same privilege to Mr. Green if within eighteen months from the date he would build a house valued at $ 300.00.

In November of the same year reference is made to a mill. "A meeting of the trustees called to consult with Mr. Pomeroy and to inspect the mill. Voted to pay Mr. Thurston fifty cents a day by the Manhattan Town Associ-

Welcome Wells, Boot and Shoe Manufacture, Manhattan is now fully prepared to make to order boots, shoes etc. Repairing done on short notice.

L. F. Woodman, Stone Mason and Plesterer, Manhattan, K. T. Business respectfully solicited and done in neat workman-like manner, charges reasonable.

H. L. Esseck, Attorney at Law. General Land and collecting agent. Manhattan.

Albert Griffin, Attorney at Law, General Land and Collecting Agent, Manhattan.

Samuel Williston, blacksmithing, Manhattan, Kansas.

W. H. Smyth, Civil Engineer and Surveyor and Deputy County Surveyor for Riley County.

And in the issue for November 5, 1859 these new

businesses were noticed:

J. D. Patterson, Clerk of United States District Court, Manhattan K. T. Land warrants bought and sold for cash and on time. Naturalisation, filing and preemption papers made out. Contested claim cases and all other business before the Land Office at Ogden promptly attended to.

Millinery---sold by Mrs. M. Miller, Kearney, Street, near the Blue Ferry, Straw Bonnets, Bonnet Ribbons, Flowers, Rooches, Black lace, Vails, Velvet ribbone etc.

George Burgoynes'---Ambrotype Picture Gallery. I would inform the inhabitants of Riley and adjoining counties that I am prepared to take correct likenesses of any size, at mode.ete charges. Gallery on Poynts, between second and third.

Hats, caps, shoes, boots, drugs, medicine, liquors, dry goods, blankets, leather goods, furniture, chairs, hoop skirts, stoves. Lewis L. Kurty, Merchant.

There appeared a number of foreign adds in every
issue advertising houses and firms in Leavenworth, Wyandotte, Kansas City, Missouri, Lawrence, St. Louis, Missouri
and New York.

In 1859 land speculation still played an important
part in daily affairs, the best claims had been taken up
long ago, but people were still buying land. In the
Express for November 5, 1859 appeared this notice.

"Caution! . All persons are cautioned against purchasing any of following described land warrants:

No. 69,448, issued to Dan Douglas for 160 acres.
No. 32,014, issued to W. Parmeter for 160 acres.
No. 61,723, issued to Grey B. Underwood for 160 acres.
No. 63,325, issued to John West for 160 acres.
No. 56,779, issued to J. B. Hincman for 160 acres.
No. 82,261, issued to Mary Barlett for 160 acres.
No. 35,868, issued to Mils Hardy for 120 acres.
No. 34,647, issued to Lincoln Fealing for 120 acres.

They have been lost or stolen from the mail, appli-
cations have been made for new issues." This notice was
published in the Express for several weeks and from time
to time these appear in later papers. Land could be
purchased at the Express office, since they acted as
general agents. On June 2, 1860 a tax of one half per
cent was levied on all real and personal property within
the city limits, payable to July 13, 1860.

In August, of 1869, one of th first travelers, Mr. Samuel Leonard, from Pikes Peak, called in Manhattan. Mr. Leonard was president of the Rocky Mount City and Colonization Office. He made the trip from there to Manhattan in eighteen days. While in Manhattan, he created a great deal of interest in the gold fields. He described the gold as being found in streams that have their sources near the mountains. At this time he had $ 4,000 in the treasury.

In 1860 the first dentist, Dr. Merriman, came to Manhattan to practice. His office was in Topeka, but he established temporary residence here for several weeks at a time, in order to serve the people of this territory.

Business competition among merchants was very keen as shown by the numerous advertisements which appeared in the papers. Especially is this noticeable in the years 1861 to 1863 due to the drought which had greatly affected the economic status of the people. Because of the hitherto prosperous years merchants had a large stock on hand and it was necessary for them to dispose of it. people had all their surplus cash invested and were unprepared for the hard times which came in 1859 and 1860. Previous to the drought people were busily engaged in gaining a

foothold in the new country. Merchants had realized this
and not increased their stock to the present proportions,
but as the people became more progressive, the merchants
had begun to expand and hope for more prosperous years
which would normally follow, as the hard times affected
all classes of people.

Lewis Kurtz, one of the leading merchants of Manhatten, who had a general store advertised "choice family
groceries, consleting of coffee, suger, teas, molasses,
cheese, dried apples, poaches, raisns, flour, salt,
bourbon whiskey, brandy and port wine for medicine and
culinary purposes. Also ready made clothing and camping
utensils." [1] This advertisment appeared at the beginning
of the hard times. In 1862, one of his adds reads, "I
have on hand an entire stock of ready made clothing of
latest style, which I will sell either for wheat, corn or
pork." [2] These two advertisment picture very vividly the
conditions in Riley County in 1862, as contrasted to 1860
and 1859, even though they have had one year's successful
cropo in 1861.

Frequently propaganda such as the following appeared
in the papers. "All the latest fashions, styles and

1. Manhattan Express, April 21, 1860.
2. Ibid, January 4, 1862.

qualities are represented in the stores of Manhattan.
Manhattan is doing a brisk business, our merchants stock
their stores on a basis of good times." 1

In 1852, business was again on the incline. At this
time the first add for a local hardware store and stove
store appears in the papers.2 Previously most of these
articles had to be purchased at the general stores or from
out of town concerns. In 1863, the first restaurant or
fruit store and eating saloon appears.3 Formerly meals
were obtained in private homes or at the hotel.

Most of the people at this time did their own work
and the employment situation was of minor importance. In
October of 1859 the first help wanted notice appears.
This calls for a girl to do general house work. Good
wages were guaranteed.4 In 1860 the office of the Express
advertised for "a first class printer not addicted to
liquor. Wages $ 12.00 a week without board or $ 8.00 with
board and lodgings.5 In 1861, B. F. Griffin advertised
for a farm hand, house girl, boy, between 14 and 18 years,
situation for a year." In the following years advertisements such as these do not appear, probably because of the

1. Manhattan Express, June 14, 1862.
2. Ibid., June 21, 1862.
3. Manhattan Independent, October 9, 1863.
4. Manhattan Express, October 29, 1859.
5. Ibid., December 1, 1860.

hard times and the war.

As early as 1854 one farmer offered to supply the people with beef and mutton. He butchered three times a week, beef on Mondays and Thursdays, mutton on Saturdays. Families would be supplied at their residences. [1]

The first market report given is for the week of January 21, 1860, at that time wheat was selling for $ 1.00 per bushel, corn $ 1.20 per bushel in the ear and $ 1.25 per bushel shelled. Oats were 40 cents a bushel, potatoes 50 cents per bushel and eggs 20 cents a dozen. Butter was 25 cents a pound, tallow 10 cents a pound, pork per one hundred pounds $ 8.00 @ $ 5.50, beef per one hundred pounds $ 4.50 @ $ 5.00. Dry hides per pound 8 cents, green hides per pound 4 cents, and a cord of wood, $ 5.00.

In February the weather was very cold and rainy and business was less active, centering chiefly on filling orders at Fort Kearney and the western portion of the county. There, butter, eggs, corn, and meal found a ready market. At this time the river was closed and navigation was impossible, but with the renewal of navigation they looked for better times. The Pikes Peak route to Denver was opened and immigrants were beginning to use it. The

---

1. *Manhattan Express*, November 5, 1859.

Manhattan Express recommended that they start from the
river towns take the boat to Manhattan, where they could
get a great part of their outfit at reasonable prices and
then proceed with their teams to Colorado.[1] Whether this
was actually followed to any great degree is very improb-
able, perhaps a few now and then outfited at Manhattan,
but it never became the commercial center desired nor was
it ever able to compare with Kansas City and Wyandotte.

The market for March 10, 1860 was the same as for
January except that wheat was up to $ 1.50 per bushel and
eggs had dropped to 8 cents per dozen.[2]

Most of the local merchants make St. Louis their
marketing headquarters, though a few go on into Chicago,
and occasionally to New York. On May 8, 1860, Mr. Curts
went to St. Louis to market. Judging from the advertisements which appear in the various papers and from the
notices of merchants going to market, St. Louis was the
distributing center for the Middle West. Goods from the
east were carried by way of the Great Lakes, the Ohio
River and the Mississippi River to St. Louis. Kansas City
began to gain in importance, but by that time, due to

1. Manhattan Express, February 25, 1860.
2. Ibid., March 10, 1860.

improved methods of transportation people were beginning to go further east and the importance of St. Louis was declining.

On May 5, 1860, the following prices were quoted, wheat per bushel $ 1.50, corn (in the ear) per bushel 20 cents, corn (shelled) per bushel 35 cents, oats 50 cents per bushel, potatoes 50 cents per bushel, eggs per dozen 8 cents, green hides 4 cents and wood per cord $ 3.50. [1]

On July 21, 1860 the following prices were quoted by Lewis Kurtz, the merchant.

```
Wheat per bushel------   ----none in market
Corn per bushel, in ear--------$00.25
Corn per bushel, shelled-------$00.30
Oats per bushel---------------none in market
Potatoes per bushel----------none in market
Eggs per dozen-----------------$00.10
Butter per pound---------------$00.10
Tallow per pound---------------$00.07
Dry hides per pound------------$00.08
Green hides per pound----------$00.04
Wood per cord------------------$ 3.50
Cheese, Kansas, per pound------$00.12
Flour per 98 pound-------------$ 5.30
Sugar, prime N. O.-------------$00.12½
Corn meal, per pound-----------$00.75
Coffee, Rio,-------------------$00.20
Tea, best imported-------------$ 1.00
Nails per pound----------------$00.08
Manilla rope-------------------$00.20
Bacon per pound----------------$00.12½
Lard, per pound----------------$00.12
Hams, per pound----------------$00.12½
Salt per pound-----------------$00.03½
Chickens(spring)per dozen------$ 2.00    [2]
```

1. Manhattan Express, May 5, 1860.
2. Ibid., July 21, 1860.

On July 23, 1860 the market remained the same with the exception that chickens had dropped to $ 1.50 a dozen.[1] The only thing there appeared to be an ample supply of and no demand for was corn. Corn had dropped from $ 1.20 and $ 1.25 per bushel in January to 25 and 30 cents in the latter part of July. In this same year George Avery and H. H. Whiting in company with some teams from Manhattan started for Denver with corn. This was the first attempt to find a western market and it proved to be successful. For years afterwards there was a great deal of freighting across the plains from this territory to Denver.[2]

In January of 1861, flour was selling at $ 4.00 per sack, shorts at $ 1.00 per 100 pounds, and bran at 10 cents per bushel, or 50 cents per 100 pounds at Lewis Kurts's store.[3] On March 29, 1862[4] L. Kurtz was offering to pay the following prices in gold for the following articles if brought in soon: Dry hides, 9 cents per pound, coonskins 20 cents, wolf skins,prarie, 25 to 30 cents, mountain wolf 60 @ 70 cents, otter at $ 1.25 and beaver, per pound washed wool 25 @ 30 cents and unwashed 20 @ 22 cents. It has been impossible to find a biogra-

1. Manhattan Express, July 20, 1860.
2. Ibid., December 21, 1861.
3. Andreas, History of Kansas, p. 1288.
4. Manhattan Express, March 29, 1862.

phy of Kurts, but he is either the leading merchant or he is making competition very keen for the other merchants.

In September of 1863, the first price list for U. Higinbotam and Company appears. They are selling Best Rio Coffee at 35 cents per pound, N. O. Sugar at 16 2/3 cents per pound, molasses at $ 1.00 per gallon, coil oil at $ 1.00 per gallon, and salt at $ 7.00 per barrel. Boots are $ 4.00 a pair. [1] George Higinbotam offers prints, muslins, and 50 cent delains, plain and figured. In his add for November 9, 1863 U. Higinbotam stated that he was willing to exchange goods for dry hides eggs, potatoes, tallow, rags, cotton, oats, and wheat. He also had on hand at that time twenty dozen hoop skirts, at all prices, 50 cents and up. [2] At this time hoop skirts were selling at Lewis Kurts's store for 75 cents.

This was a good time for stock raisers and sheep raising was looked upon as one of the most profitable. [3] There was plenty of pasture and Kansas was a good grain country. In 1864, Mr. Dyke of Ogden[4] bought twenty yoke of four year old, unbroken steers at the rate of $ 70.00 per yoke. People were gradually beginning to realize that

1. Manhattan Independent, September 14, 1863.
2. Ibid., November 9, 1863.
3. Ibid., November 15, 1863.
4. Ibid., February 8, 1864.

there was money in this business.

During and immediately following the years 1859, and 1860, money became very scarce. In November of 1861, the following notice appeared in the paper. "All persons indebted to the firm of John Pipher and Company, will please bring in their cash, wheat and corn immediately, and settle up accounts, as we cannot allow them to run indefinitely." 1

In 1862, Lewis Kurtz published a notice saying he would take Riley County script for ready made clothing.[2] He was also selling a number of articles at cost. In 1861, he had already signified his willingness to take Missouri money at part for goods and to redeem all his one dollar bills in gold or good eastern funds.[3] Even fresh butter and eggs were accepted by him in exchange for goods.[4] There was a great number of forced sales and law suits.[5]

As early as 1859, business on the levees was declining, partially due to the cold weather and because people rather mistrusted the river during the winter season. In the winter of 1859, there were "three boats

1. Manhattan Express, November 23, 1861.
2. Ibid., July 12, 1862.
3. Ibid., November 23, 1861.
4. Ibid., May 11, 1861.
5. Western Kansas Express, August 17, 1862.

lying at the landing, one flat boat and two skiffs, all
sunk."[1]

In a letter from one of the local merchants to the
Express he discusses the river traffic in the past two
years, 1858 and 1859, when there had been practically no
river traffic. There had been some talk of building boats
but none had been constructed during that period.

The first talk of a mill was recorded in the Secretary's book in 1855. The next mention is in 1861 when a
notice appeared in the Western Kansas Express, which said
that a flour mill was on its way to Manhattan and construction would begin in a about two weeks. Due to the
scarcity of money, Mr. Barnes proposed to grind for a toll,
in order to enable the farmers to have their wheat ground.
This mill was delayed and was not shipped until February
of 1862,[2] and the manufacture of flour did not begin until
May of 1862. This mill was one of the best in Kansas at
this time.[3] It was needed and was very successful. The
Express describes it as "having an immense business.
There is no end to the amount of grain waiting the milling
process. A superior quality of flour is manufactured

1. Western Kansas Express, December 24, 1859.
2. Manhattan Express, February 15, 1862.
3. Ibid., May 17, 1862.

here." [1] In February of 1864 the rates for grinding wheat
were raised to 15 cents a bushel because of the price of
wood and labor. Also the expanding business.[2] In June of
1864 the price was again raised, this time to 20 cents a
bushel.[3]

During these years the northern part of the county
around Randolph was developing and in 1862, John S.
Randolph offered to any person who would establish a steam
saw mill at that point, 1,000 logs to commence with, all
the wood that was needed to run the mill, free use of a
blacksmith shop and a house to live in. There was no mill
within twenty mile of Randolph. [4]

In this same year a soap factory was established in
Manhattan, the first of its kind. All new industries were
heartily encouraged.

Fort Riley furnished a ready market for Riley County,
a place to buy and sell. On May 26, 1860, there were sold
at auction between thirty and forty horses and one yoke of
oxen.[5] This was an excellent opportunity for the farmers.

From time to time contracts such as the following
were printed and submitted to the people. "I will receive

1. Manhattan Express, August 5, 1862.
2. Manhattan Independent, February 8, 1864.
3. Ibid., June 15, 1864.
4. Manhattan Express, January 4, 1862.
5. Ibid., May 19, 1860.

proposals to furnish the post of Fort Riley with beef for
one year commencing July 1, 1860. Beef to be supplied in
accordance with terms of contract which may be had on
application. Bids close at ten o'clock, June 23. W.
Ransom Jr., 1st Cavalry. [1]

On July 18, 1862, Fort Riley wanted five hundred tons
of hay and asked the farmers to supply it. [2] In 1863, bids
were received for 8,000 pounds of bacon sides, fifty head
of beef cattle, 40,000 pounds of flour and 20,000 pounds
of potatoes. [3] At times additional labor was needed and
the farmers were given an opportunity to earn some ready
money. In 1864, 300 teams were wanted to haul hay from
Fort Leavenworth, and 80 mowing machines were also wanted.
They would pay from $ 4.00 to $ 6.00 per day and parties
were to haul 10 tons or more. [4] These opportunities meant
a great deal to the people. Money was scarce and hard to
get and working for the government or serving as supply
agents assured them of their money.

In the years to follow there was not a great change.
Growth and development were gradual. True, even here there
had to be some readjustment after the war, but it did not

1. Manhattan Express, May 26, 1860.
2. Ibid., July 2, 1862.
3. Manhattan Independent, August 17, 1863.
4. Ibid., August 15, 1864.

seriously disturb the economic life. Things went on much
the same as before until the railroad became a factor.
This brought up an entirely new problem, and one which
took years to work out harmoniously.

Transportation

In the early years of Riley County history, as in the
history of every pioneer country, transportation was entirely undeveloped. Travel was by foot or on horse back
and as far as improvements were made they were mostly
local. Poyntz Avenue, the main street of Manhattan, was
macadamised in 1859. This was the first attempt of its
kind in Riley County.

River traffic did not hold up long due to the fact
that the river could not be depended on. It was constantly rising and lowering and many of the early steamers were
grounded. Most of the early settlers came to Riley
County by steamer until about 1857, and after that most of
the travel was overland. Occasional trips were made up
and down the river to the year 1860, and even then it was
suggested as a means of travel to Pikes Peak, going by the
river to Manhattan and overland from there on. [1]

---

1. Manhattan Express, February 25, 1860.

In 1869, the Manhattan Express stated that business on the levee had been poor, due to mistrust in the river and the climate. At that time most of the boats were lying idle and a letter from one of the local merchants to the Express, March 10, 1860 stated that in the last two years there was practically no river traffic, though there was some talk of building boats.[1]

On June 16, 1860, it was stated that the Big Blue and the Kansas Rivers had been rising rapidly during the past twenty-four hours and it would be a good time for the new Wyandotte steamer to make her trial trip to Fort Riley. After this river traffic at Manhattan readily declines and there is only occasional mention of it.

In 1860, the local pony express had again established a regular time, and by October of 1861, a mail schedule was established which was posted in the post office and published in the paper.

Manhattan City Post Office
Arrival and departure of mail.

Topeka, Leavenworth, Atchinson, and East.
Arrives———Tuesday, Thursday, and Saturday, 5½ P. M.
Departs———Monday, Wednesday, Friday, 7 A. M.

---

1. Manhattan Express, February 27, 1860

Post office open 6 A. M. to 9 P. M.
Sundays 9 to 10 A. M. and 12 to 1 P. M. [1]

The United States Express Company, established a line
from Leavenworth to Junction City which was to make semi-
weekly runs.[2] The Transcontinental Express did not go
through Manhattan.

In 1861, a bridge was built across the Big Blue.
This was the first bridge to replace the government
bridge at Juniata which was destroyed in 1856. The
purpose of this bridge was to complete the highway over
the river at Manhattan, to accommodate the Pikes Peak
travel.[3] In 1862 there was again fear that the bridge
would be destroyed. There were twenty inches of ice on
the river and they thought that when winter broke, the
immense pressure of the floating masses would destroy it.[4]
During the winter, due to the heavy ice, teams and people
crossed the river on the ice. There is record of several
teams breaking through while attempting to cross.[5] In
1862 the ferry across the Blue at Manhattan was free,
probably because of the completion of the bridge and
people preferring to use it.

1. Manhattan Express, October 20, 1861.
2. Topeka Tribune, June 9, 1861.
3. Western Kansas Express, April 20, 1861.
4. Manhattan Express, February 8, 1862.
5. Ibid., February 15, 1862.

Various pioneer trails went through Riley County.
Among them were the old Fort to Fort trail established in
1852, the Smoky Hill Stage route and the Butterfield
Overland Dispatch. The latter followed the Smoky Hill
route from Leavenworth to Denver.

As early as 1858, Pikes Peak became the leading
trail of Kansas.[1] The Manhattan to Denver road was first
considered in September, of 1859. A town meeting was
called to discuss the need of a road to the Colorado Gold
mines.[2] In 1860 the Express office had a number of in-
quiries asking for information regarding the best road to
Pikes Peak. On April 6, 1860, the subject of locating a
road to Denver from Manhattan was before the city council.
Green Russell, the famous mountain pioneer made the
following proposition to the people. That for $ 3,500 he
would locate the road over what was known as the Smoky
Hill route.[3] In May of 1860, the people of Manhattan met
at the city hall to hear the Smoky Hill route discussed.[4]
In June, of 1860, $ 500.00 was apportioned to Manhattan
as the sum they were to raise toward building the road
from Leavenworth to the "gold regions of Western Kansas."

1. Wilder, Annals of Kansas, p. 188.
2. Manhattan Express, September,24, 1859.
3. Ibid., April 7, 1860.
4. Ibid., May 25, 1860.

City bonds were to be issued by the mayor and register,
made payable on or before October 1, 1860. Also a special
tax levied on all city property by the city marshall. The
bonds issued were to be receivable in payment of the
special tax levied.[1] Surveying was done and work finally
begun on the road. By May, 1861, large trains of cattle
had passed through Manhattan on their way to the gold
regions.[2]

Another important element in the settlement of the
country was the system of land grant railroads. "Agitation was begun, looking toward the building of railroads from Leavenworth to Fort Riley, with the primary
purpose of having improved transportation facilities between the two military posts on the western frontier. As
early as August 30, 1856, the legislative assembly of
Kansas Territory passed an act incorporating the
Leavenworth, Pawnee and Western Railroad for construction."[1] The projectors did not organize for more than
a year and for a long time failed to interest capital in
the enterprise. The first railroad ever laid in Kansas
was put down at Elwood, opposite St. Joseph, Missouri in

1. Manhattan Express, June 2, 1860.
2. Western Kansas Express, May 18, 1861.
3. Kansas Historical Collection, O. P. Byers, How railroading and Did the Wild West Stories. Vol. IV,
   p. 000-000.

1860, but drought and the war intervened to prevent extensive building in Kansas at that time.[1] Surveys were made from Leavenworth and Wyandotte in the spring of 1863, after the Pacific Railroad Act of July 1, 1862, became a law.[2] "This act authorized the Kansas company to build from the mouth of the Kansas River, where it connected with the Pacific Railroad of Missouri, to a connection with the future Union Pacific Railroad at the one-hundredth meridian." [3]

The recognition thus given the Leavenworth, Pawnee and Western project, by the National government, readily attracted promoters and capitalists. "The policy of subsidizing the railroads in land and bonds, by the general government, was diligently labored for by Kansas men at Washington. In 1863, Congress made to the State of Kansas, a grant of land, giving alternate sections, one mile square, ten miles in width, amounting to 6,400 acres, a mile on either side of a proposed line running from Atchinson or Topeka, to some point on the southern or western boundary of the state in the direction of Santa Fe, with a branch on the southern line of Kansas to[4]

1. Noble L. Prentis, The History of Kansas, p. 124.
2. Byers, When Railroading Outdid the Wild West Stories, p. 240.
3. Ibid., p. 240.

Mexico City. This grant was transferred to the Atchinson, Topeka and Santa Fe Railroad, February 1864 and amounted to some 3,000,000 acres of land.[1]

In May 1863, the Leavenworth, Pawnee and Western project passed into the control of Samuel Hallet and General John C. Fremont and became the Union Pacific. Trouble arose and Fremont was bought out, John D. Perry, President of the Exchange Bank of St. Louis taking his place and financing the project.[2] The first forty miles were completed in June, 1865 and extension westward began. January 1, 1866, the first section of the line was opened for traffic extending from Kansas City to Topeka and a branch from Leavenworth to Lawrence was next. It was begun on May 15, 1866. Wamego, Manhattan, Ogden and Fort Riley were successive stages, each being the western terminus until Junction City was reached on November 12, 1866.[3]

Surveys of the Kansas Central Railroad were in progress as early as 1859 and by August 14, 1859, they had gone as far as Topeka. Engineers were planning to cross the river and located[4] the road on the north side by

1. Noble L. Prentis, History of Kansas, p. 194.
2. Byers, Op. Cit., p. 860.
3. Ibid., p. 861.
4. Western Kansas Express, August 20, 1859.

the way of Manhattan. This was of great interest to
people and the farmers who were raising cattle expected
it to overcome the difficulty of no close markets. By
the latter part of December, 1859, the Central Railroad
was looked upon as a fixed fact. It would connect the
cities of Wyandotte, Lawrence, Topeka and Manhattan. In
January of 1860, the discussion of the project under
deliberation was presented to the City Council with a
view to obtaining from our city "certain bonds for a
large sum of money to be devoted toward helping the construction of a railroad from the Missouri River to Manhattan." [1] The newspaper took a favorable attitude toward this project, as being worthy of support and one
greatly needed by our city. It considered the railroad
as a "vital necessity to our present and future prosperity." [2] It would increase our commerce, agriculture,
help and the general moral and the political and social
advancement of our people. The people were urged to vote
for the project, should it come before them.

In July of 1860, a railroad grant to Kansas, by the
National government was defeated, due to the inability of
Kansas men in Washington to agree on a route. Each one

---

1. Manhattan Express, January 21, 1860.
2. Ibid., January 21, 1860.

wanted his home town to be the railroad center.[1] At that
time there was talk of calling a railroad convention of
all parts of the territory to decide on a plan. A
district convention was held at Manhattan, September 20,
1860 to elect a representative to the general convention
in Topeka, October 17, 1860.[2] The state convention in
Topeka succeeded in adopting a schedule of railroads that
they believed would effectively develop the resources of
Kansas and connect it with all the grand trunk railroads.[3]
One of the officers of this convention was C. F. de
Vivaldi of Manhattan, editor of the Express. The convention determined to present a memorial to Congress asking an appropriation of public lands to aid in the construction of several railroads. Among these one of the
railroads was to go from the city of Wyandotte (connect-
ing with the P. and G. Railroad and the Pacific Railroad,)
up the Kansas valley by way of Lawrence, Lecompton,
Tecumseh, Topeka, Manhattan and Fort Riley to the western
boundary of the territory. About one hundred twenty-five
delegates were present from various counties at this convention.[4]

1. Manhattan Express, January 21, 1860.
2. Ibid., September 2., 1860.
3. Western Kansas Express, October 20, 1860.
4. Wilder, Annals of Kansas, p. 343.

In 1861, the railroad question was of vital importance and the fourth representative district, in their party platform made it a political issue by saying, "Let no man be elected to represent Kansas in the United States Senate who does not stand pledged in purpose and interest to promote the advancement of Kansas and of the Leavenworth, Pawnee and Western Railroads." [1] Another question which arose at this time in this connection was what system of railroads should be advanced and whether government aid should be employed to advance the sectional interest and whether the railroad or the whole state should participate in the benefit of congressional land grants. This question was considered to determine how leading substantial interests of the country were to be affected.[2] On April 26, 1862, it was announced that the Leavenworth, Pawnee and Western Railroad Company planned to begin work the following month. A treaty between the company and the Potawatomie Indians was ratified by the United States, thus giving the company, 350,000 acres of land.[3]

In August of 1862 a public meeting was held to discuss western interests. Resolutions were passed against

1. Western Kansas Express, March 3, 1861.
2. Did.
3. Did., April 26, 1862.

measures of the Leavenworth, Pawnee Railroad Company, in
causing land for fifteen miles on each side of the proposed track up this and the Republican valley to be with-
drawn from preemption, sale and private entry.[1]

   This is the last mention we find of the railroads in
the newspapers during the period this paper discusses.
The war becomes the absorbing topic, railroad construction
is dropped. Both men and capitol are needed elsewhere
and the drought had taken most of the latter. During the
years 1863 to 1865 the war and advertisements consume
every inch of space in the newspapers. The war because
it is the chief interest and the advertisements, because
they are a source of money. For the years 1865 to 1866
the files are very incomplete and no mention of the railroads is to be found in the few papers obtainable. The
war and reconstruction still appear to be the dominant
objectives. It is known that the railroad had reached
Manhattan by November 1866, but it has been impossible to
find the exact time. In 1866 the National government was
still making grants of land within Kansas to the railroads,[2] and in 1867, there were only 523 miles of railroad in Kansas. The Kansas Pacific was within thirty-five

1. Manhattan Express, August 19, 1862.
2. Wilder, Annals of Kansas, p. 436.

miles of the western boundry, completing three hundred
thirty-five miles of the main line.

The history of Kansas railroads is so interwoven
with the history of the development of the state that it
is difficult to determine its contribution as a separate
factor. "Kansas was really a laboratory for the testing
of the practicability of railroads in developing a new
and savage country." [1] After the railroads had been extended and built into Kansas, the wealth and population
began to multiply rapidly. New problems arose to con-
front the people on every side. Whether or not it was
entirely due to the railroads was hard to say, but they
were a factor of great importance and must be given
proper consideration.

CHAPTER V——SOCIAL DEVELOPMENT

Education

The people of Manhattan displayed an early interest
in the social side of their life and education was a
major phase. A public school was established almost
immediately after settling of the town. Of course the
very earliest part was done in the home and many of the

1. Williamson, Harold Arthur, The Effect of Railroads on
        the Development of Kansas in ——, Manhattan,
        Kansas, 1930.

people who settled here had a very liberal education.

By the time the first newspaper came to Manhattan
the schools were well established and had been running
several years. The first school building in Manhattan
was where the Junior High school now stands. It was
built by the city, but furnished by the people of the
town. The first school was taught by Miss Vance, a paid
school teacher, also an Episcopalian. The Methodists
objected to this and got Amanda Arnold to start a paid
school, however this school didn't continue long.

The first article to appear in the newspaper in
connection with the school was one discussing the Manhattan City School and education. The free schools are the
most beneficial, progressive and enlightened system or
institution of our age. On April 1, 1880 the free schools
of Manhattan in charge of Miss Adelia Sewell, gave an
exibition of the progress made by the pupils during the
last two terms. "All children, elegantly dressed,
numbered about forty, seated on a platform, ornamented
with evergreens and flowers, which stood before the
audience. The youngest must have been about four, the
oldest not more than fourteen." [1]

---

1. *Manhattan Express*, April 7, 1860.

In 1860, Mrs. A. R. Kermott opened the first music
school in the city. It was held at her home on Wattier
Street. Instruction was given in instrumental and vocal
music at $ 12.00 per term of twenty-four lessons. Pianos
and melodians could be procured at five per cent in advance of manufacturers prices.[1]

On April 5, 1862, the annual exibition of scholars
was again held.[2] The meeting was at the Methodist Church,
in charge of Miss Bewell who was still the teacher. The
people of the city seem to be very much interested and
greatly concerned about education and interested in its
advancement. The same month another school program was
given. "Dialogues on different subjects, well selected
pieces of prose and poetry and other exercises of character, were delivered by the children, all of them speak-
ing in their turn with ease, precision and evident marks
of intelligence. The singing between mental exercises
was good and Mr. E. D. Norton receives credit because it
is hard to conduct a chorus of little ones." [3]

On April 19, 1862, a notice appeared in the paper
stating that the spring term would begin the following

1. Manhattan Express, May 19, 1860.
2. Ibid., April 5, 1862.
3. Ibid., April 7, 1862.

Monday. Children living outside the city limits were
required to pay a tuitition fee of $ 2.00 in advance. [1]
On August 25, 1862, the school committee met to consider
applicants for the city school. They were examined by
the committee, on their qualifications as teachers and
general knowledge. [2]

On October 20, 21, and 22, 1863, a teachers institute was held in Manhattan. All the teachers in the
county were invited. The State Superintendent of Public
Instruction and several other prominent speakers were
there and a general discussion for the benefit of the
teachers was held. [3] At the present time Teacher's Institute for the county meets before the opening of the term.
If this was followed then it is immediately apparent that
the terms opened much later then than now. This is
probably true, since according to the Manhattan Express
the second term for the year 1862, did not open until
April 21, 1859.

By 1864, the educational institution of the district
had grown so much it was necessary to hire another teacher. Miss Sarah Kimball was hired as the assistant teach-

1. Manhattan Express, April 7, 1862.
2. Ibid., August 12, 1862.
3. Manhattan Independent, September 25, 1865.

or to take care of the additional number of pupils.[1]

As early as 1869 the importance of home education is
recognized. The following article appeared. "Whatever
defects there may be in home education it is certain that
the exceptions are rare where the moral training of the
mother is not according to her best capacity for the
benefit and advantage of her off spring. Her influence
is often counteracted by the habits and examples of the
father, but in such cases she is not responsible if her
care and teaching are of no avail. Home education, where
parents are united in sentiment, leaves its impression
upon the mind and heart which can never be totally ob-
literated. The principal cause of departure from the
path of right is associations. The poor mother engaged
in her house-hold affairs, dependent upon her labor for
her livelihood, has little time to devote to her
children; and as soon as they are able to walk by themselves they seek playmates and the youthful mind is
readily impressed for good or evil according to the
disposition of the association. The effect of those
impressions is more lasting in most cases than the influences, and examples of the parents. If children were not

---

1. Manhattan Independent, April 26, 1864.

early less subject to such influences, there would be
less vice in the world. Home education is the best for
the youthful mind. The most determined man in every
situation of his life will, to the latest period of his
pilgrimage be influenced by the early teachings of his
mother, if the example and the habits of the father are
in unison with her council and instruction." [1]

In 1859 the Manhattan Express calls the attention of
the people to the news depot of Mr. Patterson, who is in
constant reception of the best magazines and periodicals
of the country." [2] The depot is at the post office.

In the summer of 1860 an art exibit came to Manhattan. At this exibit landscape and scenes, painted by Mr.
Gardner the artist were on display. Mr. Gardner depicted
scenes, phases of emigrant life and Norman life. These
were painted for exibit in the east and were displayed
here by Mr. Gardner on his way back east. The people
seemed to think this was a very unusual opportunity and
one to be taken advantage of. [3]

In 1862, the first mention of the public library
appears. At that time the librarian of the Manhattan

1. Manhattan Express, October 20, 1859.
2. Ibid., September 17, 1859.
3. Ibid., July 21, 1860.

Institute had secured the use of a room in the Manhattan
House. Books belonging to the library were placed there
and the people were asked to return all books borrowed,
also to give any of their private collection they desired. Before the small library club had maintained a
library in private homes. The entire movement was an
outgrowth of the Manhattan Institute, organized to provide worthwhile entertainment for the young men of the
community.[1] Literary discussions were held and there
were regular reading meetings.

According to the Secretary's Book of Bluemont
Central College, when George S. Park visited here in
1858, he located the town site "with special view to the
erection of an institution of learning, of a high grade
and having in particular an agricultural department."[2]
Shortly afterwards a group of five individuals of liberal
education, located a second town site at about the same
place. These separate interests had the same end in
view and consolidated.

It is known that the two groups located the said
town site, but whether or not they had in mind the

1. Manhattan Express, November 28, 1861.
2. Secretary's Book of Bluemont Central College, p. 1.

building of an agricultural college when they chose the
town site, is very doubtful, though romantic. "However
in 1857 the Bluemont College Association was chartered to
build a college at or near Manhattan under the manage-
ment of the Methodist Episcopal Church." [1] The College
trustees received a large number of Manhattan town lots
as a donation to the enterprise and a considerable a-
mount in personal solicitations here and in the east. A
farm was obtained and a three story building erected in
1859, on a hill a mile west of the present college
building. The Manhattan Express for October 1, 1859,
describes it as a splendid three story stone edifice fast
approaching completion. At that time the masons work
was finished and the carpenters were working. They considered the building should be ready for school by
December 1, 1859.

According to the issue of the Manhattan Express,
for October, the Methodist Episcopal Church , "was one
of their best projects and should be one of their best
schools in the west." [2] On December 24, 1859, Manhattan
College, the term here applied, was on the eve of completion. The trustees had decided that it should be

1. Andreas, History of Kansas, p. 1308.
2. Manhattan Express, October 1, 1859.

opened for reception of students during the first week of
January, and that the Reverend Washington Marlatt should
instruct the pupils.

The Manhattan College opened January 8, 1860 for the
first time. Reverend Marlatt assisted by Miss Julia C.
Bailey furnished the instruction.

Tuitition per term of 11 weeks.

Common English branches---------------$ 3.00
Higher English branches, as philosophy, physiology,
  algebra etc.----------------$ 4.00
Language-------------------$ 5.00

Tuitition in advance.

Necessary text books in hands of treasure at low rates

Further information can be obtained by writing
  President, Professor I. T. Goodnow. [1]

On January 27, 1860, notice appeared that the first
annual catalogue of the college was on sale at the
Express office. The price was 10 cents per copy.[2]

The spring term of Bluemont College opened April 16,
1860. The same teaching staff was employed and the same
fees were charged.

In December of 1861, the college bell was first
elevated to its lofty position. It was a gift of Joseph
Ingalls of Massachuestts and the same bell that still

1. Manhattan Express, January 21, 1860.
2. Ibid., January 27, 1860.

rings here each morning and noon at the present time.[1]

In 1863, because of lack of funds the Bluemont
College was offered to the State to be converted into a
State School, in accordance with an act donating public
lands to several States and territories which may provide
colleges for benefits of agriculture and mechanical arts.
Kansas was given 90,000 acres of land. This was acted
on by the legislature in 1863 and accepted.[2]

The first term as organized by the authorities of
the State began September 2, 1863, and continued for
thirteen weeks. Plans were made to organize a music
department.

```
Common English branches were-----------$ 4.00
Higher English, Algebra, Geometry, Language etc.------
    $ 5.00.
Music on the
    Melodeon------------$ 8.00
    Piano-------------$10.00
Incidental expense for fuel, sweeping and bell ring-
    ing------------$00.50
Special exercise in riding on horseback, calesthenics,
    gymnastics etc.-----------given without charge.
Board in private families-------$ 2.00 to $ 3.00 per
    week. [3]
```

The name of Bluemont College was changed to the
Kansas State Agricultural College and a meeting of the
board of regents of the college was held July 23, 1863.

1. Manhattan Express, December 21, 1861.
2. Andreas, History of Kansas, p. 1365.
3. Manhattan Independent, August 17, 1863.

Issac T. Goodnow, Superintendent of Public Instruction
was chairman.[1] By December 7, 1863, seventy pupils were
enrolled in the Kansas State Agricultural College.

In February 1864 a proposition was made to run an
omnibus from the town to the college twice a day to carry
and to return students morning and evening.[2] By March
it was decided that Mr. Alfred A. Perkerson was to run
the bus. It was to leave the Manhattan House 8:30 A. M.
and return at the end of the days classes.[3]

During the winter of 1864 several public lectures
were given at the college and one of the fivet was a
lecture on Electricity given by Professor Issac T.
Goodnow.[4] In 1865 regular lectures were given at the
college by the president and his assistants.[5]

As early as 1861, the location of the State University was one of the leading questions. At that time
a bill to locate it at Manhattan passed both houses of
the State Legislature, but was returned unsigned by the
governer.[6]

In 1862 the agitation between Topeka, Manhattan and

1. Manhattan Independent, August 17, 1863.
2. Ibid., February 22, 1864.
3. Ibid., March 21, 1864.
4. Ibid., March 21, 1864.
5. Ibid., February 14, 1865.
6. Western Kansas Express, June 1, 1861.

Lawrence over the State Univ rsity was still causing a
great deal of trouble. people of Manhattan urged that
since the buildings were already here it should be located here.[1] On January 25, 1862, an editorial appeared in
the Express trying to sell the idea to the people in the
surrounding country. By February of the same year
Lawrence and Emporia were both petitioning for it. Manhattan still claimed that due to her buildings it should
be here. At that time they still belonged to Bluemont
College and they offered to turn them over to the State.[2]
In March a bill to locate the University at Manhattan
failed to pass the senate in spite of the work of members
of this part of the country.

In September of 1862, an editorial appeared in the
Express, which stated that the reason they did not support Isaac T. Goodnow for State Superintendent of Public
Instruction was because they feared it would be antago-
nistic to the people. The State University was the chief
question and the people knew that Manhattan wanted it
and that Goodnow was intensely interested. The paper
was afraid that due to his interest he would cause enemies instead of friends even though he was well quali-

1. Manhattan Express, January 19, 1862.
2. Ibid., February 1, 1862.

fied.[1] It was some time before this question was
settled and then the University went to Lawrence. Manhattan finally succeeded in obtaining the Agricultural
College. Education was just one of the many elements in
the social development of the people at this time which
dominated their lives.

Morals and Law Observance

The early settlers of Manhattan were greatly concerned about the moral welfare of the community. The
purpose of the Manhattan Institute and other similar
organizations was to provide wholesome amusement and
further the intellectual development of the people. The
newspapers cooperated in carrying out this purpose. In
the first issue of the paper an article appeared laud-
ing up right men. "We love upright men. Pull them this
way or the other, and they only bend, but never break.
Trip them down and in a trice they are on their feet
again. Bury them in the mud an in an hour they would be
out and bright. You cannot keep them down, you cannot
destroy them. They are the salt of the earth, who but
they start any noble project? They build our cities,

---

1. *Manhattan Express*, September 8, 1862.

whiten the ocean with their sails and blacken the heaven
with smoke of their cigars. Look to them, young men and
take courage. Imitate their example and catch the spark
of their energy." 1

In the issue for October 29, an article appears in
regard to the home. "Six things are requisite to create
a really happy home: Intregrity must be the architect,
and tideness the upholsterer. It must be warmed by
affection and lighted by cheerfulness, and industry must
be the ventillator, renewing the atmosphere and bringing
in fresh salubrity day by day; while over all, as a protecting canopy and glory, nothing will suffice except the
blessing from above." 2

Such articles as "an inordinate desire to obtain
possession of secrets is an unerring indication of inability to keep them," 3 and "mother, teach your child
to wait upon itself, to put away a thing when done with
it, but do not forget you were once a child. The grief
to little ones is too often neglected; they are great
for them. Bear patiently with them, and never in any
way arouse their anger if it can be avoided"   appears

1. Western Kansas Express, August 20, 1859.
2. Manhattan Express, October 29, 1859.
3. Ibid., October 29, 1859.
4. Ibid., December 1, 1859.

quite frequently. "Fun at home" was emphasized as a means of keeping morale of youth high. [1]

Most of the papers carried a front page story with a very pointed moral and such tittles as "Misdirected Revenge," "The Self Sacrifice," "Whining," "Hints to the Young Gentlemen," and "Pride."

Every attempt was made to keep the community orderly and law abiding yet discropencies did appear and misdeeds were frequent. March 24, 1863, this article appeared. "On Wednesday evening last about dusk a man named Hardesty, confined in the jail in this city, broke out of that institution and 'got up and dusted.' A company of men started on Thursday morning in pursuit, but we think the individual has rather too much of a start." [2]

Various attempts at horse thievery were made around Manhattan. Two horses were taken June 10, 1860, from a Mr. Dodge and an unsuccessful attempt was made to take two from Dr. A. Hunting. The thieves were scared away. [3]

Lewis Kurtz, merchant, submitted the following notice. "A fine black cassimere hat with low crown, edge of rim trimed with satin patent leather band, size

1. Manhattan Express, December 10, 1859.
2. Ibid., June 10, 1860.
3. Ibid., May, 26, 1860.

about 6 3/4, little worn by the subscriber, was taken
from my store on Thursday eve between four and six o'-
clock. The person is requested to return the same, and
there will be no questions asked, otherwise he will be
dealt with according to the law, as he is known."

For some time the country around Manhattan was dis-
turbed by the depredations of a gang of lawless men, who
engaged in the business of runing off hereos, stealing
and "all things not pleasing to a respectable community."
These men were a great nuisance, and in order to rid the
community of them a citizen's meeting was called to be
held at the court house at 2:00 o'clock, March 24, 1860.
The purpose was to device a means of protecting the property of citizens from the vagabonds who were annoying
them. [1]

In July of 1860, the sheriff of Morris County offered $ 80.00 reward for the apprehension of one Thayer,
alias Smith, who shot his wife. He was last seen going
to Junction City from Riley. [2]

John Fisher, a Manhattan merchant, on his way to
Atchinson for goods had two horses stolen from him, but
these were recovered about thirty miles from the place

1. Manhattan Express, March 24, 1860.
2. Ibid., July 21, 1860.

where they were stolen. [1]

Manhattan also had a small number of more serious
events touch its community. In July of 1860, John Mc
Gram, a young man in the employee of the Manhattan Gas
Company, "went on a spree." Later he went to Kansas City
and while there took arsenic. [2]

One of the few shootings in Manhattan occurred when
a man from Pikes Peak, Munroe, who was drunk, shot Newton
Barber, injuring his limb, the ball lodging in his feet.
This grew out of Munroe's wanting to pour whisky down
Barber's neck while he was being shaved. Barber knocked
the glass out of Munroe's hand, cutting his forehead.
Friends of Barber thought the dispute had been peacefully
settled, but a short time later the shooting occurred. [3]

An event of great local interest occurred when Mr.
Vivaldi was attacked by Mr. W. H. Smythe. Vivaldi was
crossing the street from his home to his office when the
incident occurred. It was believed to be due to Mr.
Vivaldi, as editor of the Express, asking Mr. Robinson to
to publish a brief statment of the disposition of a
relief fund of $ 100.00 which Mr. Robinson had received. [4]

1. Manhattan Express, July 28, 1860.
2. Ibid., July 28, 1860.
3. Ibid., September 22, 1860.
4. Ibid., March 16, 1861.

In November of 1861 the Deputy U. S. Marshall
arrested one of the noted horse thieves, E. W. Brach, a
few miles from Manhattan.[1] This was the beginning of an
open war on "jayhawkers." In December a number of jayhawkers were arrested who had been especially active in
thivery and plundering. They were arrested while running their acquired stock to places of safety outside of
town. "Vile whiskey added to this, made these men danger-
ous to the countryside. They glorified in their crimes
and defied civil authority. While making the arrest one
man was shot in the head and died immediately."[2] Six
were arrested with the one killed. Manhattan was put
under military control until Monday.

Jayhawking continued, even though military authorities had been put in charge. Cloveland, the most
notorious coamp, and his gang were still at large. The
people felt that the military authorities were not doing
their part and that, if they had waited for them to
furnish protection, they would have been wiped out some
time before.[3] In May, of 1862, Cloveland was finally
captured and put to death by General Burt, a government

1. Manhattan Express, November 30, 1861.
2. Ibid., December 14, 1861.
3. Ibid., April 12, 1862.

official. [1]

Quantrell's raid did not directly affect the citizens of Riley County, yet it aroused a great deal of sympathy among the people here for the people of Lawrence. [2] A relief committee was formed in Manhattan to send aid to Lawrence and to render all possible services. [3]

The week of September 7, was one of excitement for Manhattan. About three o'clock Wednesday morning, men were summoned to appear at the militia headquarters armed. Messengers from Fort Riley had arrived saying Quantrells were ranging the Neosho country. This was evidently false, since no attack was made. Nevertheless, all places of business were ordered closed from 4:00 to 6:00 P. M. and all able bodied men were to present themselves on parade for drill. [4]

The trial of John Brown, produced a great deal of interest, but little comment among the people. The papers followed it closely, but did not take, as far as the newspaper was concerned, partisan views. [5]

The Temperance Union was a very active and important society in Manhattan at the time the paper came to the

1. Manhattan Express, May 17, 1862.
2. Ibid., August 23, 1863.
3. Ibid., September 14, 1863.
4. Ibid., March 24, 1863.
5. Ibid., November 26, 1859.

community. It was organized here in 1858.[1] The first
notice of it appears in the issue of the Express for
December 19, 1859, when it was noted that a Temperance
meeting would be held "in the name of the Western Star
Division No. X of S. of T. on Tuesday, December 13, 1859,
in the Congregational Church.[2]

That there was need for such an organization is
shown by the following quotation: "Quite an interesting
'set to' occurred in our town last Wednesday, between a
couple of young bloods. From slight misunderstanding,
originating in too free use of the ardent, the lie was
passed, and after considerable swearing, cussing, etc.
they 'peeled and went in.' A few blows were sufficient
to put their eyes in mourning and place upon their faces
sundry 'Fourth of July'..., when the parties were sepa-
rated, taken before his honor, the mayor, and 'diddled
to the tune of $ 5.00 and costs.' "[3]

On April 17, there was a State Temperance meeting
in Topeka. The people of Manhattan were very much interested and were urged to attend.[4] As a rule the meetings
were held at the various homes[5] but in March of 1862, a

1. Andreas, History of Kansas, p. 1307.
2. Manhattan Express, December 10, 1859.
3. Ibid., March, 1861.
4. Ibid., December 24, 1859.
5. Ibid., November 23, 1861.

general meeting was held in the Congregational Church
and "friends and enemies were invited to attend." Selections from the Evening Temperance Advocate were read.[1]

In February of 1862, and again in June of the same
year the city passed an ordinance to regulate the sale
of intoxicating drugs. This was to be enforced by the
city marshall. A licence was required to sell them.[2]
From time to time articles such as the following would
appear. "Tis' little trouble to brew beer, but beer
brews much trouble." [3] In December the Express said,
'There had been a lull in the temperance movement for
the last few months' and the devil had gotten in his
work. It appealed to the people to put an end to it.[4]

In February of 1864, the first bill regulating the
sale of intoxicating liquor appeared before the legislature of Kansas.[5] At that time the people opposed it
fearing that such a bill would increase the vice. In
March of the same year there was a citizens meeting to
revive the temperance union.[6] Shortly afterward a notice
to the effect that Mr. G. A. Parkinson made a nice arti-

1. Manhattan Express, March 28, 1862.
2. Ibid., February 8, 1862.
3. Manhattan Independent, August 10, 1863.
4. Ibid., December 21, 1863.
5. Ibid., February 8, 1864.
6. Manhattan Independent, March 24, 1861.

ale of Root Beer appeared and it was suggested, that the
people substitute it for the stronger beverages they had
been using.[1]

In the first issue of the paper, August 20, 1859,
a petition for divorce appears.[2] And these reappear from
time to time at infrequent intervals. They were not un-
common, but were looked upon by the people with disap-
proval and dislike.

In writing this paper it has not been intended to
depict a sordid view of Riley County. The community was
really much freeeer from vice and crime than Junction
City and many similar communities surrounding it. Then
as now a history traced through the newspapers pictures
more or less of the yellow side, since that is what
furnished copy for them. It is only occasionally that
the better and brighter side is brought to attention.
We knew that the people were really concerned about the
welfare of the community and were endeavoring to make it
of the highest type, with high type of moral and law
abiding citizens.

Religion

1. Manhattan Independent, May 25, 1864.
2. Manhattan Express, August 20, 1859.

The religious life of Manhattan was one of its
earliest considerations and one given immediate attention.
Reverend Bleed and his settlers came here with that purpose in mind and all of the early founders were deeply
concerned with this phase of their life. As early as
1854, services were held at the Dyer home at Juniata.

Methodist Episcopal services were first held on
board the steamer Hartford about April 30, 1855. They
continued after reaching Manhattan and in 1857 the first
Methodist Church was erected.[1] The next church to be
located here was the Congregational church. It was the
second church of this order to be established between the
Missouri River and the Rocky Mountains. The first services were held April 22, 1855, in a tent erected,[2] for
that purpose. Contributions from people of the east
gave the church a good start. Among the people con-
tributing to this church were: Stephen A. Douglas,
Abraham Lincoln and Owen Lovejoy.[3] The third church to
be organized in this community was the Protestant
Episcopal or St. Pauls, which held the first service in
July, 1857, and in May, 1858 a parish was organized.[4]

1. Andreas, History of Kansas, p. 1306.
2. Ibid., p. 1306.
3. Ibid., p. 1306.
4. Ibid., p. 1307.

On August 14, 1858 the first services of tno Baptist
Church were held. It continued as an active-body until
November 13, 1860, when it became an incorporated organization.[1] In July of 1857 the Presbytrian Church was
organized, though services were held as early as 1856.[2]
The next religious organization was the Methodist
Episcopal Colored Mission organized in 1858.[3] After
this a number of new religious demonations and organizations appear to become a part of the life of the
people of this community.

In the issue of the Express for August 20, 1859, a
notice appeared which stated tnat the First Baptist
Church held services regularly at the scheel house at
10:30 o'clock, every Sunday morning.[4]

In January of 1860, a resolution passed by the
Congregational Church and society acknowledged the
reception of $ 500.00 from the American Congregational
Onion and several donations made by individuals and
churches of the east and of the est for the erection of
a church here. Also a vote of thanks was given to
George W. Underwood of Michigan for the gift of a clock.[5]

1. Manhatten Express, April 21, 1860.
2. Ibid., May 11, 1861.
3. Ibid., April 28, 1860.
4. Ibid., July 14, 1860.
5. Ibid., January 4, 1862.

The Methodist Episcopal Church was dedicated on
April 15, 1860, at 11:00 A. M. [1] All the different religious societies in the town were represented. The
church was of white limestone, with the pews and woodwork of native black walnut. [2] The choir was under the
direction of Mr. M. D. Horton and the organ music was
furnished by Mr. Charles Barnes Junior. In 1861, a new
pastor, Reverend J. T. Auld came to Manhattan to begin
his work. [3]

In 1860 one of the first Episcopal conventions of
the Diocese of Kansas met in Topeka to elect a Bishop.
Representatives from Manhattan were present and took part
in the meeting. [4]

In 1860, a camp meeting was held on the farm of Mr.
Thompson, three miles southeast of Manhattan. This
meeting began on July 19. "Brethren in the ministry and
members from surrounding charges" were invited to attend
and meet there. It was stated that there was a good
supply of water, wood and pasture convenient to the
ground, and a large attendance was anticipated and hoped
for. As was stated in the Express, "Come brethern and

1. Manhattan Express, April 7, 1860.
2. Ibid., April 21, 1860.
3. Ibid., May 11, 1861.
4. Ibid., April 28, 1860.

elsters and let us worship God together in the tented grove for a few days." 1

On December 29, 1861, the Riley County Bible Society held its annual meeting at the Methodist Church. The object of this meeting was to see that every family in the community had a Bible. 2

This gives a fairly clear picture of the early religious activities of Riley County. It is known that in the next few years the churches grew and prospered, but because of the war being the chief consideration the papers neglect to give mention to the churches and their activities. The next church to be organized was the Church of the Disciples in 1872 and 1873. 3 After that several new churches come into the community and play rather an important part.

The church furnished much of the social life and activity and plays rather a major part in daily affairs. This will all be discussed under the Social Life of the community and the part it has in every day affairs will be discussed.

Political Growth to 1866

1. Manhattan Express, July 14, 1860.
2. Ibid., January 4, 1862.
3. Andreas, History of Kansas, p. 1306.

Kansas, while still an unorganized territory, caused
a great deal of political strife, which finally resulted
in the Kansas-Nebraska Bill of 1854. This bill caused
both free and slave people to enter Kansas. The great
majority of the latter came over from Missouri and did
not make permanent settlements. Most of the free-staters
came here and settled permanently and came with the expressed purpose of saving Kansas from slavery. [1]

During the years of 1854 to the early part of 1861,
Kansas was a territory. From 1855 to 1859 the people of
Kansas were so busy gaining a foothold in the soil and
getting themselves permanently established, that political development of their own was neglected. There was
interest in national politics, but there were no newspapers or means of keeping the people well informed.

From the first the people were dominantly Republican in sentiment. The first declaration of their
intention to organize politically appeared in the Manhattan Express, September 17, 1859. At this time all
citizens who were interested in the formation of a Republican Club were invited to meet at the court house,
Tuesday evening at 7:00 o'clock. At that time the first

1. Goodnow, Personal Reminiscences and Emigration, p. 342.

meeting was held, and the Republican Club officially
formed. [1]

On September 30, 1859, a Republican convention was
held in Ogden to elect delegates to attend the State
convention. At this convention the Riley County delegates chosen were G. F. de Vivaldi of Manhattan and B.
B. Edmonds of Ogden. They were to be the representatives at the State convention, to be held at Topeka
October 12. [2]

On the first Tuesday in October, 1859, the
Wyandotte Constitution was submitted to the people to
vote on. All male persons, white, who were twenty-one
or over and citizens of the United States, and all
persons of foreign birth who had declared their intention to become citizens, were allowed to vote. [3]

On September 16, 1859, there was a meeting at the
Methodist Episcopal Church. Governor Charles Robinson,
who was visiting in Manhattan, talked on why the people
of Kansas should support the Wyandotte Consititution
and gave a review of the reasons of Democratic oppo-
sition. [4]

1. Manhattan Express, September, 24, 1859.
2. Ibid., October 1, 1859.
3. Ibid., September 17, 1859.
4. Ibid., September 19, 1859.

In the issue of the Express a copy of the Wyandotte consltitution was printed so that all the people might read it and become familiar with it. A copy of the Osawatomie Platform appeared at the same time, also a registry of the voters of Riley County. [1]

General Pomeroy addressed the people of Manhattan at the Methodist Church. His subject was the Wyandotte constitution. At this time the attitude of the people toward General Pomeroy appeared to be very friendly and he was held in high esteem and looked upon as a leader in Kansas affairs.[2] At this time the Express predicted that Kansas would soon become a State and cease to be bleeding Kansas.[3]

On September 24, 1859, another copy of the Osawatomie Platform appeared, and a statement, apparently by the editor, that Kansas had, since the organisation of the territory been controlled, both in the legisla- tive and executive departments by the Democrats. The affairs and welfare of Kansas had not been fostered in the proper manner and it was recommended that they should be turned over to the Republicans. [4]

1. Manhattan Express, September 17, 1859.
2. Ibid., September 24, 1859.
3. Ibid., September 24, 1859.
4. Ibid., September 24, 1859.

The Express of October 1, 1859, urged the people of
Riley County to vote for the Wyandotte constitution and
through the paper the following heading appeared, "Vote
for the Constitution," meaning the Wyandotte constitution.[1] The Express was to receive all returns for the
election in regard to the vote on the constitution and
on the home-stead law, and volunteered to keep the
people notified.[2] All free-state men of Kansas were
urged to vote at the October election which was to decide definitely whether Kansas would be slave or free.[3]

On December 10, 1859, the following article appeared in the Express. "Admission of Kansas into the
Union by the people of Kansas and a complete set of
State officers elected under it. Congress has decided
in her favor. The question now is whether she will be
admitted to the United States during the present session
under her present constitution. Congress is under the
control of the Democrats and they may oppose Kansas being admitted because she is a free State. The Democrats want the presidential election of 1860 and Kansas,
whether in or out of the Union will exert a great influ-

1. Manhattan Express, October 1, 1859.
2. Ibid., October 8, 1859.
3. Ibid., October 26, 1859.

ence against their candidate." [1] Following this article
arguments were put forth attempting to prove that the
admission of Kansas into the Union would be best for the
Democrats.

In November, 1859, the second Republican Club was
formed in Riley County. This was at Ogden. Before this
the people of Ogden had been very active, but this is
their first organized effort. [2]

On April 28, 1860, a copy of "The Kansas Admission
Bill" as passed by the Senate and House of Representatives appears on the front page of the Express. In May
a statement appeared to the effect that the House had
passed three important measures, The Homestead Bill, the
bill to supress polygamy and the Kansas Admission Bill.
They were then waiting for the decision of the Senate
and the president. The support of all Republicans was
urged as being needed for most worthwhile causes. [3]

On June 9, 1860, the Express stated that the Kansas
Admission bill which passed the house by a large majori-
ty April 11, was virtually killed in the United States
Senate, being postponed to no definite date. [4] Buchanan

1. Manhattan Express, November 5, 1859.
2. Ibid., November 5, 1859.
3. Ibid., May 12, 1860.
4. Ibid., June 9, 1860.

vetoed the homestead bill and the two most important
issues which had one time soon considered as passed had
failed.[1] Discontent was very apparent and the papers
were filled with political propoganda.

On Monday, December 24, 1860, the bill for the
Admission of Kansas to the Union again went before the
House. The papers predict.d that this time it would
probably pass.[2] It was again postponed till January 7,[3]
and did not pass the Senate until January 21, 1861.[4] On
February 1, a meeting was held at the city hall to "greet
and celebrate the intelligence of our admission into the
Union."[5] Senator elect S. B. Huston of the 4th district
was present and addressed the meeting. By March 30,
1861, the first legislature of Kansas was in session at
Topeka.[6]

The election of the Senators to represent Kansas in
the United States Senate did not create much of a stir.
General James H. Lane and General Pomeroy were elected.[7]
After the election the editor of the Express became
rether doubtful about the election of Pomeroy, feeling

1. Manhattan Express, June 30, 1860.
2. Ibid., December 2., 1860.
3. Ibid., January 3, 1861.
4. Ibid., January 24, 1861.
5. Ibid., February 1, 1861.
6. Ibid., March 30, 1861.
7. Ibid., April 13, 1860.

that he might hinder the cause of Kansas. [1]

In January of 1862, there was State legislation against jayhawking[2] and in June of the same year two State officers were impeached.[3] There was some difficulty at this time because the governor did not want to appoint new officers to fill these vacancies.

In July of 1862, the question arose as to whether or not the State should avail itself of the offer of the General government to receive the bonds of Kansas to the full amount of the direct tax,[4] which at this time would be most burdensome. This was immediately following the two seasons of drought and the people felt that at this time they could not support such a measure.

On July 15, 1862, the people of Riley County met with the Senator and Representative of this district to discuss with them the "doings" of the last legislature and to instruct them in regard to the will of the people.[5]

In the first issue of the Western Kansas Express the Homestead bill was taken up and discussed. The question was discussed whether or not it should be or would be a part of the constitution of Kansas. At this time the

1. Manhattan Express, April 13, 1861.
2. Ibid., January 23, 1862.
3. Ibid., July 28, 1862.
4. Ibid., July 22, 1862.
5. Ibid., July 26, 1862.

newspapers were asked to support the measure. They feared the Democrats would oppose it because it would curtail
the credit system, which the majority of the people feel
is already too large. It appealed to the business men
on the ground that it would locate more homes in Kansas
and give them more trade, to the mechanics, saying it
would give them greater or more work and to the Republicans because it will give them greater power.[1] In
May, 1862, the Home-Stead bill passed both houses and
was signed by the president.[2] And in the June 7, issue
of the Express a copy of the bill was printed. This
bill was looked upon as a great boom to freedom by the
people of the west. [3]

The year for the presidential election was 1860,
and the people of Kansas were very interested. The
Democratic convention was called to order at Charleston,
South Carolina, April 23, 1860. [4] An attempt was made
to nominate a candidate, but without success. The delegates of the convention were divided and they had split
over slavery. Part of the delegation wanted to support
Douglas and popular soverignity, others were for

1. Western Kansas Express, August 30, 1859.
2. Manhattan Express, May 24, 1862.
3. Ibid., June 7, 1862.
4. Ibid., April 28, 1860.

Jefferson Davis and slavery. They agreed to adjourn and
meet again June 18, at Baltimore, Maryland. [1] The convention was generally spoken of as a farce. They had
adopted the same platform as that of 1856. [2]

In January of 1860 president Buchanan sent out a
mess'ge to the people. It was printed in the Express
along with an apology of the editor for forcing the long
message of the president on them. He was critized very
severly. From the editorial it was very evident thet he
was not entirely pleasing to the people, at least the
people of Kansas and that they did not approve of his
attitude. He had critized the people rather unjustly
and they felt that it was the Democratic party that de-
served the critism. [3]

On May 12, 1860, the first notice of the impending
Republican convention appeared. The probable Republican candidates eere discussed and their respective ages
given. Among these were:

William Seward, 59 years old, born May 16, 1801, New
York.

Salmon P. Chase, 52 years old, born January 13, 1808,
New Hampshire.

---

1. Manhattan Express, May 5, 1860.
2. Ibid., May 12, 1860.
3. Ibid., January 7, 1860.

Abraham Lincoln, 51 years old, born February 12, 1809
Harden, Kentucky. [1]

This convention was to meet in Chicago, June 13, 1860.[2]
A later issue sets the date as Wednesday, the 19, of May
as opening date.[3] Five solve states and all the free
states were to be represented. The aim was the triumph
of Republican principles.[4] This convention nominated
Abraham Lincoln for president and Hannibal Hamlin of
Maine for vice-president.[5]

The nomination of Lincoln for president met with
the approval of the people. Through his administration
the newspapers support him and encourage and urge the
people to do the same. Vivaldi, appeared to be a great
admirer of Lincoln and to understand and have a great
interest in politics. From now until the end of the
Reconstruction period the greater amount of copy in the
Manhattan papers is given over to Lincoln and to the
war. During the year 1860, each copy of the paper carried a Lincoln for president and Hamlin for vice-
president notice, with a rather lengthy discussion of
their fitness and ability.

On May 9, 1860, the Union convention of the old

1. Manhattan Express, May 12, 1860.
2. Ibid., January 28, 1860.
3. Ibid., May 12, 1860.
4. Ibid., May 19, 1860.
5. Ibid., May 12, 1860.

line Whigs and Know Nothing parties was held. They
adopted the platform, "The Union and the Constitution."[1]

This was the first hint or notice of the fact that
there might be a division in the Union, up to this time
it had been ignored or unseen. As time passed, it was
very easy to recognize that they, the people, had made
the chief issue of the campaign a moral issue. Slavery
stood out unparalleled, above all issues.[2] In the
issue of the Express for October 20, 1860, appeared an
editorial "Disunion." The South at that time were
threatening to break up the Union ever the slavery
question and the nominztion of Lincoln. By November
socession was being discussed with considerable warmth
and much ability. South Carolina was at that time the
center of agitation. Even then the people of Kansas,
as the following article shows, did not realize fully
just how serious it was. "While we do not believe that
the present threatening aspect of the cotton states will
result in anything which will be likely to endanger the
stability or permanence of the Federal Government, we
are of the opinion that an investigation should be made.
That States possess the abstract right of cession we

1. Manhattan Express, May 12, 1860.
2. Ibid., October 13, 1860.

cannot doubt." [1] In December the "Irrepressible Conflict grew warmer" the eleven States were becoming more united and more insistent upon the institution of slavery. [2] Later there appeared a discussion of the "value of the Union" and an article on "California against Secession." [3]

In December 20, 1860, South Carolina's State convention declared itself in favor of secession, following a debate on the adoption of secession ordenance.

In 1861 Lincoln took office as president and this greatly increased the high feeling in the South. In the issue for March 9, 1861, Lincoln's presidential address was published accompained by many articles of praise.

A very interesting case appeared in Kansas during this year, in which slavery was upheld. A man attempted to reclaim a slave and brought it to court. Judge Peterson who was presiding, decided in his favor, saying that a law prohibiting slavery in Kansas was unconstitutional. [4]

By January 1861 it was realized that war was inevitable. The United States Arsenal at Baton Rouge had

1. Western Kansas Express, November 24, 1860.
2. Ibid., December 1, 1860.
3. Ibid., December 22, 1860.
4. Ibid., January 5, 1861.

surrendered and Florida and Alabama had seceeded. [1] By
February 16, 1861, six States had seceeded: South
Carolina, Florida, Alabama, Mississippi, Georgia, and
Louisiana. [2]

On June 1, 1861, an editorial on "Our Government"
appeared. It urged the people to stand back of their
government. They were needed and the government was
deserving. They also asked that in the coming Congressional election the people preserve the Union by elect-
ing members to Congress who would work with Lincoln and
support him.[3] Throughout the war Lincoln was given the
support of the people of Kansas and of Riley County.
In the early days of the war Mr. Vivaldi went to Washington to visit. While there he joined the army and
was later appointed consul to Santos, Brazil by President Lincoln. During the war the major part of the
paper was taken up with war news, various campaigns and
battles. On February 22, 1864, a notice appeared to the
effect that on that day Lincoln was to issue his procla-
mation of Universal Emancipation.[4] By March, 1864, [5]
the Riley County papers were beginning again the old

1. Western Kansas Express, January 26, 1861.
2. Ibid., February 10, 1861.
3. Ibid.; June 8, 1861.
4. Ibid.; February 22, 1864.
5. Ibid., March 7, 1864.

campaign cry, "Lincoln for president." For the years
1865 and 1866 many issues of the paper are missing. We
know that they did relate the fact of Lincoln's death
and mourn with the rest of the nation, but the copies
which deal with this phase of our nations history are
missing.

During this period little mention is made of local
and state affairs. Everyone is too tensely interested
in the nations struggle. On September 14, 1861, a note
was made of the coming state election to decide where
the state capitol would be located, and Manhattan, along
with every other town in the State was cited as the
ideal place.[1] By October, though still a vital question
to the people here, the idea of locating the capitol
here had been dropped. The town was considered to be
too far west, and Lawrence and Topeka became the con-
tending points. Manhattan threw her support to Topeka
in hope that she might get the State University here. [2]

The banking law was another issue which was submitted to the voters and one of the last issues, outside of the State University to be mentioned.[3] Every-

1. Western Kansas Express, September 14, 1861.
2. Manhattan Express, October 19, 1861.
3. Ibid., October 26, 1861.

one, Republican and Democrat was dominated by the war
and the reconstruction after the war. Then as now Riley
County was largely Republican and her destiny was in the
hands of a few political leaders.

Social Life

Looking at the social life of the people of Manhattan as portrayed by the newspapers they appear to be
one big family. Up to 1859, when the first paper was
issued, there is no way of tracing the social life of
the community in any definite form, but when it is followed through the next seven years, it is very easy to
picture the Thanksgiving services, the Christmas parties
the fourth of July picnics, and the numerous school
programs and church fairs as forming a very important
part in these years from 1859 to 1866.

In the Manhattan Express for November 26, 1859, the
following notice appeared. "Thanksgiving day in Manhatten. This day of joy and prayer was generally ob-
served in our community in the true spirit of its
institution. A union religious meeting was held in the
Congregational Church, where the resident pastors of
the Methodist Episcopal, Congregational, and Baptist

Churches conducted together the services of the day.
The sermon was preached by the Reverend Mr. Kermott of
the Baptist Church." [1] The people of the various
joined services on this day every year. [2]

The Christmas celebration as portrayed by the
papers was looked upon with due reverence. "Tomorrow is
the anniversary of the birthday of the Savior of the
World, a day consecrated by holy customs of ages of
religious observances and social rejoicing. As it falls
on Sunday, the religious part of the ancient usage will
be performed in all our churches, Episcopal Methodist,
Congregational and Baptist, where appropriate services
will be held at 11:00 o'clock A. M. The social rejoicing will be held the following day." [3] This gives us a
hint as to the active part the churches played in the
lives of the people.

At the same time it was noted that Messers Ed
Duvall and George Wiemer were getting up a ball and supper, to be given Monday evening, January 2, 1860, at the
Peoples hall in Manhattan. Extensive preparations were
made and it was to be "one of the grandest entertain-

1. *Manhattan Express*, November 26, 1859.
2. *Ibid.*, November 30, 1861.
3. *Ibid.*, December 24, 1859.

ments ever given in Manhattan." The Manhattan string
band was to furnish the music, with such "solo-string"
music as they produce, for a "gay assembly of those who
delight to 'trip the light fantastic.' " [1]

On June 30, 1860, the following Fourth of July
celebration was arranged. It was to take the form of a
Sunday school picnic, in charge of the officers of the
various schools, with program arranged.

Officers

President————————————————————Dr. Whitehorn
Chaplin————————————————————Reverend C. R. Blood

Order of Exercises

Prayer————by chaplin
Singing————by children
Reciting of the Declaration of Independence————by
  James Humphrey
Singing the National Aire————by choir.
Address————by Reverend J. Paulson to the
  parents
Singing————by children
Address to the Sunday School————by Reverend M. V.
  Preston
Singing————by choir.
Popular Address————by Reverend W. J. Kermott
A General sing
Refreshments
Toasts and Sentiments

It was expected that each family would supply them-
with the necessary amount of refreshments. The Sunday

---

1. Manhattan Express, December 24, 1859.

Schools were to meet at the Methodist Episcopal Church
at 9:00 o'clock A. M. and from there were to go to Mr.
T. J. Roosa's grove. Everyone was invited to attend. [1]

That evening a 4 [th] of July dance was given at the
Peeples hall and about seventy-five couples attended,
many of them from neighboring towns. [2]

Washington's birthday was celebrated by the ladies
of the Methodist Church holding services in his honor
and an entertainment was held at the college. [3]

The annual 4 [th] of July picnic was held at the
grove on the banks of the Blue. The program was much as
the previous year, with a patrotic and religious service
followed by dinner, speeches and patrotic songs. [4]

During the winter of 1862, social parties became
more numerous, so much so that the Express saw fit to
mention it. "Social parties are becoming quite numerous among us this winter. We notice our citizens are
enjoying themselves in this way to an unusual degree.
We consider it a good omen and hope that friendship and
good will will continue to be cultivated among us. [5] It
also mentioned that Christmas that year was attended

1. Manhattan Express, June 30, 1860.
2. Ibid., July 7, 1860.
3. Manhattan Express, February 25, 1861.
4. Ibid., July 6, 1861.
5. Ibid., January 4, 1862.

with the usual festivities. "The gay and merry ushered
in its welcome dawn with a festive dance at the Stone
Hotel, while smiling faces of little ones told plainly
that good Santa had not forgotten them." [1] A Masonic
festival was held at the school house which was largely
attended and described as a fine affair. Following this
festival, the next important event was the annual fourth
of July picnic.

In September, arrangements were being made for the
State fair, in Leavenworth. The citizens of Manhattan
took a very active part in this. There was to be a
Stock Auction, ladies exhibition and a Colorado Premium
and Target shooting.[2] The date of the fair was October
6, 7, 8, and 9. This was the first State Fair to be
held in Kansas.[3]

On December 7, 1863, a public meeting was held at
the Methodist Church at which Governor Carney was the
chief speaker. The people of Manhattan and community
appeared to be very fond of oratory.[4]

Plans for the annual fourth of July picnic of 1864
were very elaborate and for the first time fire works

1. Manhattan Express, January 4, 1862.
2. Manhattan Independent, September 14, 1863.
3. Ibid., September 28, 1862.
4. Ibid., December 7, 1863.

were mentioned. Mr. A. A. Parkonson had a large as-
sortment consisting of Rockets, Roman candles, and
Indian fire crackers. If fire works were a part of
previous celebrations they we.e not mentioned, and
judging from the papers, this is their first appearance.[1]

Fairs, given by the ladies of the various churches,
were another important element in the social life of the
community. In November 1859, the ladies of the Protestant Episcopal Sewing Society of Manhattan, held a fair.
All people were invited to attend. "A sumptuous entertainment and many rare articles to attract the eye were
to be found on their tables.[2] On February 14, 1862, the
ladies of the Methodist Church held a fair at the
College building. Articles were on exhibit and to sell.
Supper was served, the price of the tickets being
twenty-five cents.[3]

Beginning in May of 1864, the first of a series of
concerts was given under the auspices of the ladies of
the Episcopal Sewing Society. The purpose was to pay
the remaining debt on the church that was then nearing
completion.[4]

1. Manhattan Independent, July 4, 1864.
2. Manhattan Express, November 5, 1859.
3. Ibid., January 25, 1862.
4. Manhattan Independent, May 2, 1864.

In the spring of 1860, juvenile concerts became quite frequent. One of the first concerts was held in the city hall, May 10, open to the public, with the admission price twenty-five cents. [1] Mr. J. D. Patterson was the director; he had formerly bought books for the children at his own expense and given them musical instruction free of charge. This shows somewhat the spirit of the people. [2] On May 11, 1862, the children of the Sabbath schools met in the Congregational Church. Singing and the recital of passages of scripture and addresses by the Reverends Beckwith, Hartford and Kermott and also by a soldier of a Wisconsin regement were part of the program. [3]

In October of 1864, a music class or singing school was formed at the Methodist Church. This was one of the first organized attempts to give instruction. [4] About $ 40.00 was made at one of these concerts. [5]

Manhattan also had several noted visiters who created quite a flurry in the social whirl. One of these was Horace Greeley, who was making a tour of the west. On his trip he made a memorandum of the diminishing comforts of life for the patrons of his Tribune, and in the list he

1. Manhattan Express, May 5, 1860.
2. Ibid., May 12, 1860.
3. Ibid., May 17, 1862.
4. Manhattan Independent, October 10, 1864.
5. Ibid., June 30, 1864.

has Manhattan, May 26, the date of his visit, potatoes and
eggs last recognized among the blessings that "brighten
as they take their flight, cheire ditto."[1] It was very
apparent that at this time he considered Manhattan the
last civilised settlement. On June 21, 1860, Governor and
Mrs. Reeder visited Manhattan. Mr. Reeder was the first
governor of the Kansas Territory.[2]

Manhattan gained some notority when Charles de Vivaldi
was appointed consul to Brazil. This event caused a great
deal of comment which increased rapidly when the assistant
editor, Mr. Humphrey brought suit against him for the sum
of $ 528.75 for money loaned and for back pay.[3]

The humor of the people lies mostly in their mode of
expression and inevent. as compared with the present day.
They had a very serious outlook on life and neglected or
did not care for many of the frivolities. Part of this
was due to the life they were forced to lead and in their
struggle for existance and part to their better judgment.
The early papers and a few of the papers during war time
carried a Humor Column, but most of the jokes and puns
which appeared in these were of the commercialized type,

1. Connelley, Kansas and the Kansans, Vol. 1., p. 98.
2. Manhattan Express, June 23, 1860.
3. Ibid., November 2, 1861.

just as they are today. The greater number of their jokes
center around married life or the attempt to gain such
bliss, politics and religion, the major elements in their
lives. The following quotations give examples. "A young
lady once hinted to a gentleman that her thimble was worn
out and asked what reward she merited for her industry.
He sent her an answer in the shape of a thimble with the
following line engraved. I send you a thimble for your
finger nimble, which I hope will fit when you try it: It
will last you as long, if its half as strong, as the hint
you gave me to buy it." [1] There is no doubt that at the
time this created a great deal of merriment, much more
than it possibly could now.

This short selected story appeared in the Express for
August 20, 1859, and was no doubt fully apreciated. It
was a take off on the Millerites and described the neglected husband and family after Mrs. Peters, the wife
joined the Millerites. She immediately began work on her
assenoion robe, feeling she would be called immediately.
Mr. Peters became very worried and finally hit on a plan.
He told his wife that after she was gone he must have a

1. Western Kansas Express, August 20, 1859.

wife to care for the family. He then picked one of her best friends and suggests that Mrs. Peters invite her over to train her. Mrs. Peters immediately gives up the idea of ascension and the Millerites and peace is restored to the family. [1] Some of their jokes would be very appropriate today and greatly appreciated by us, such as:

"We hope the debating club at Topeka will not consume
the substance of the people of Kansas, by much
longer prolonging their useless wrangling." [2]

And another which is very applicable to present day conditions.

"I think I have seen you before, sir; are you not
Owen Smith? Oh yes, I'm Owen Smith and Owen Jones,
Owen Brown, and Owen everybody." [3]

At the time this appeared the Kansas drought was at its height.

In the Express for November 26, 1859, rather an amusing comment appeared on a book entitled "Woman a Hundred years, Hence." "He must be a bold man who will attempt to predict what women will be then. Will she wear crinoline and small bonnets, or will she have invaded the sphere of man, donned the b--loomers and taken possession of the presidents chair." [4]

---

1. Western Kansas Express, August 20, 1859.
2. Ibid., April 20, 1860.
3. Ibid., May 18, 1861.
4. Ibid., November 26, 1859.

This vivid description was given of the dancing in
Washington, in 1860. "The want of variety in the metro-
politan dancing, was fully made up by fancy things, such
waltz and poka. These were absolutely barbarous. The old
fashioned waltz, the morality of which, oven Bryon called
in question is here ignored as altogether too cold and
distant. The lady lays her head on the gentleman's bosom,
puts her hand in his and the other in his coat tail pocket,
and resigns herself to his embrace, and goes to sleep, all
but her feet, which, when not carried by him clear off the
floor, go patting around on the toes. The gentleman, thus
entwined, throws his head back and his eyes up, like a
dying calf; his body bent in the shape of a figure 4, he
whirls, backs up, swings around, and swoons to all appear-
ances, dashes forward and leaves the ring to the delight
of all descent people." [1]

Considerable attention was given to fashions and
quotations from various parts of the country appear. Then
as now Paris appeared to be the index. "Parisian Fashions.
As hoops once get out of fashion, so they will again fall
into disuse. The latest fashion bulletin from Paris which
describes the modes for July, announces two facts, highly

1. Manhattan Express, January 21, 1860.

interesting to most female society, double skirts to be
discontinued, in consequence of the change of mode just
beginning, which only permits a great width to the lower
part of the dress, thereby diminishing the proportion of
the upper. Invasion on rights of long triumphant crinoline. Empress Eugenie, who rules fashion in Paris, is
against excess crinolines. She is inclined to bring back
fashions of early part of Empire when Josephine was the
autocrat of dress, and restore the figure to its natural
shape. Short waists were to be revived." [1] This short
bit of advise followed the above quotation. "Not good for
short stumpy women, who we predict will cling to extradori-
nary crinolines, remarkable double skirts, mutilated
flounces and wonderfully long waists." [2] From time to
time advertisements appear which announce or advertise
"Madam Demorests' Mirror of Fashions," "a fashion magazine, patterns accompaning each magazine; no young lady
can afford to be without it." [3]

Various crazes and fads appeared here, as they are
bound to in any locality, but one of the most highly advertised and most amusing was the mysteries of the Crescent

1. Western Kansas Express, August 20, 1859.
3. Ibid., August 20, 1859.
4. Manhattan Express, May 3, 1862.

and Pot Hook dialect. "Persons desirous of obtaining an insight into the mysteries of the Crescent and Pot Hook dialect, commonly turned Phonography, were invited, on paying $ 3.00 to become a member of the class formed by Professor J. D. Patterson, who could be consulted at the Postoffice at all times or at the meeting of the class which met Thursday night at the People's Hall.[1] Frequently the name of J. D. Patterson appeared in various sections of the paper and it is very probable that he was a resident of Manhattan.

The Manhattan Institute was responsible for much of the entertainment furnished the people during these years.[2] It early became an established organization and conducted very worth while programs, having debates, spelling bees, lectures, group reading, and encouraging individuals to read. It also entertained with socials and fairs.

The Kansas State Agricultural Society was another of the early organizations. This was formed in March, 1862,[3] for the advancement of agriculture, to encourage the people, to discuss new fields and for social purposes. At that time almost every organization served as a social

1. Manhattan Express, January 21, 1860.
2. Ibid., January 12, 1861.
3. Ibid., March 22, 1862.

organisation and the purpose for which it was originally
intended.

To me the social life and interests of this community seem very high, and the people show an unusual concern.
The lawless element was well under control and every
opportunity was taken to advance the intellectual and
moral welfare of the community. Most of the social activities of the community were tied up with intellectual interests, either through the schools or the churches, and they
all seem to work together for the benefit of society. A
most altruistic attitude was taken by the entire community. And as for the individuals, they appeared to be very
concerned about the development of their better self. The
life of Riley County was very harmonious and well ordered.
The people made it fit the definite pattern they had intended for it. However during the middle sixties the war
interrupted a share of the social activities, which it
took the community several years to regain.

CHAPTER VI—RILEY COUNTY AND THE CIVIL WAR

The first talk of war seemed to come as rather a
shock to the people of this community. Even while the
discussion of the secession of South Carolina was raging

the Express, expressed the belief that the "threatening
aspect of the cotton States" would not result in anything
likely to endanger the stability of the Union. [1] They
realized and recognized the fact, that slavery was the
chief moral issue of 1860, but not as a power capable of
breaking the Union. [2]

On April 28, 1860, the first real mention of slavery
was made by the Express, in an article "Twin Relics of
Barbarism" in which Mr. Owen Lovejoy was exalted for
publishing an anti-slavery newspaper. Even then slavery
had to share its honors with poligamy, these being the
"Twin Relics of Barbarism." In this article slavery was
attacked on a moral basis and because of frequent attempts
to plant it in the North and in territories.

In the October 20, issue of the Express, an article
on "Disunion" appeared, stating the South was threatening
to break up the Union because of slavery and the nomination of Lincoln for president.

On January 5, 1861, the Express stated that Fort
Moultrie and Pinkney Castle had surrendered to the militia
of South Carolina. And at this time the president was

1. Western Kansas Express, January 5, 1861.
2. Ibid., January 12, 1861.

condemned for not strengthing the forces there and supporting the commanding officer. A report that the president feared assassination was also published. At this time a doubt was still expressed about this secession movement, stating that as yet it had not taken practical shape in resistance to the laws of Congress.[1] On January 4, the United States Arsenal at Mobile was taken, followed by the rumored capture, of Fort Morgan.[2]

In April of 1861, the long threatened hostilities between the United States and the Confederacy commenced. Loyal States were responding to the presidents calls[3] in the North and in the South. At that time the border states were looked upon as being in sympathy with the south.

The war in Kansas was but a continuation of the border troubles,[4] the people were open to exposure from attack by the Indians and the Missourians. It assumed the character "of a war of revenge, of ambushes and ambuscades,...of swift advances and hurried retreats, of stealth, darkness and murder."[5]

War news consumed the greater part of every news-

1. Western Kansas Express, January 5, 1861.
2. Ibid., January 12, 1861.
3. Ibid., April 20, 1861.
4. Franklin, Noble L., History of Kansas, p. 88.
5. Ibid., p. 88.

paper, from 1861 to 1866, when the reconstruction was the
chief problem. Campaigns and battles were told and retold.
Dispatches were printed at length and the one consuming
thought of the people seemed to be the war. Slow as to
the realisation that such an event was really possible,
after it was once determined they entered the conflict to
give it their full support.

By April 27, 1861, Fort Sumpter had been stormed, to
be followed by the taking of Harper's Ferry arsenal. [1]

In the April 27, issue of the Express a call to arms
appeared. Citizens of Manhattan and Riley County were
requested to meet at the City Hall in Manhattan, April 30,
1861, at 2:00 P. M. to organise a military company and to
prepare for threatened emergencies. "Let patriots rally
and defend their flag." This order was issued by James
Humphrey, mayor of Manhattan at that time.

By May 4, 1861, the Fifth Regiment was organised
composed of companies from Riley, Clay, Davis, Dickenson,
Saline, and Ottawa Counties. [2] Two of these companies wore
organised at Manhattan, one a company of infantry under
Captain A. B. Spinney, and a company of cavalry under A.

1. Western Kansas Express, April 27, 1862.
2. Ibid., May 4, 1861.

F. Head called the "Manhattan Greys" [1]

Mr. C. F. Vivaldi, who had gone to Washington, had enlisted in General Lanes Company, [2] which at that time was defending Washington. This was prior to his appointment as consul to Santos, Brazil.

By May 11, 1861, a company of forty-three men was organized at Ogdon. This company chose the name of the "Riley County Mud Sills." [3]

By June 1, 1861, Missouri had decided to remain in the Union. [4] This stopped a great deal of the border warfare and gave the people renewed confidence, because from that time on they did not have the invasion of a Southern army from Missouri to worry about.

By March 15, 1862, the third company had been formed at Manhattan since the war began and at that time the paper stated that perhaps Manhattan had contributed more men than any other place of the same number of inhabitants in Kansas. [5] This statement may or may not have been true, but it was entirely possible.

In July of 1862, the war pressure was again brought to bear upon the people. During this time it was played

1. Western Kansas Express, May 4, 1861.
2. Ibid., May 4, 1861.
3. Ibid., May 4, 1861.
4. Ibid., June 1, 1861.
5. Manhattan Express, March 15, 1862.

up more by the paper and a call for 300,000 more men was
issued. [1]

In September of 1862, a recruiting and mustering
office was established at Manhattan and more men were
needed. This is the last call for men that appears in
Riley County papers. Late in 1864, Manhattan organised
another company, but they never saw action. Manhattan and
Riley County were through the war always able to furnish
more men than they were asked for and this was true for
the entire state of Kansas.

During the latter part of the war when the soldiers
were beginning to return home some of them disabled for
life a number of their stories appear in the papers, also
a number of letters written home by the soldiers, many of
whom saw active service in the North and in the South and
played very important parts in the war. A few were known
to be in Shermans and Lane's army.

After the war Riley County settled down to a routine,
similar to that before the war, with the exception that
then it was necessary to do more work to make up for the
time lost. Prices had been good during the war, but man
power had been cut down and this slowed down production.

1. Manhattan Express, July 12, 1862.

One old settler, told the following story. During
the winter months of the war, a guard was kept day and
night to protect the people from Indian attacks. At that
time he was the only able bodied man in the community of
Manhattan, and because of defective hearing he had not
been accepted. He kept watch at night to relieve the
older men and let them have day duty. If there was an
attack, he was to give the alarm to arouse the community.
During the winter months when the nights were much longer
this duty was very trying, and the guards which were to
relieve him were often late. This particular morning they
were exceptionally late and after waiting several hours
past the time they were due he sounded the alarm. Immediately the whole community was awake and ready for
attack when they came out. Whether the people were disap-
pointed at having this false alarm given was not stated.
It had served the desired purpose.

Through the war Manhattan nor any part of Riley
County was ever attacked, though occasionally the people
heard that war parties were headed their way. Their part
was to supply the men and food and their contributions
in both served to help the cause of the Union.

CONCLUSION

In conclusion I wish to state that the material for this paper has been gathered from the Riley County newspapers or to be more definite from the Western Kansas Express, the Manhattan Express, and the Manhattan Independent, the only newspapers existing in Riley County up to 1866.

Parts of this paper appear to be and are rather brief and sketchy, and do not portray a clear or definite trend of events and happenings. Especially is this true for the years from 1864 to 1866. From this time on there are many issues of the paper missing. The file in the State Historical Library at Topeka is not complete and it was impossible to find the missing issues, or a treatment of the economic and social development in any other source for this period. Occasional references were taken from the Topeka, and Leavenworth papers, but local communication at that time was very poor. The interest of the people either settled on their immediate locality or on affairs of the National Government.

On looking back at the preceeding paper, I realize that Riley County was settled by a very high minded and enlightened group of people, who throughout their lives,

worked and struggled to give it those qualities and things
with which it is endowed today, and have taken so little
effort on our part. In this respect I believe it was
superior to other pioneer communities. There seems to be
less strife and less trouble here than in most communities. Peace, prosperity and progress seem to have joined
hands with the people in making this community an ideal
place in which to live.

ACKNOWLEDGMENTS

The writer wishes to express her appreciation and
thanks to Professor R. R. Price, Dr. F. A. Shannon and
Professor M. C. Cowell for the helpful suggestions and
criticisms which they have offered in the preparation of
this thesis; and to the late Mr. Bacon, librarian in the
newspaper section of the State Historical Library; and to
the librarians of the Kansas State College of Agriculture
and Applied Science for the help and courtesies which were
extended to her in the use of materials and facilities of
the library.

LITERATURE CITED

Primary Sources

Secretary's Book of the Manhattan Town Association, Book No. 1. Records and Constitution of the Boston Association April 3, 1855 to June 29, 1855 and the Manhattan Town Association, July 7, 1855 to January 7, 1856.

Secretary's Book of Bluemont Central College.

Newspapers

Leavenworth, The Kansas Weekly Herald, September 15, 1854-1859.

Leavenworth, Kansas Territorial Register, July 7, December 22, 1854.

Manhattan Express or Western Kansas Express, August 20, 1859-1862.

Manhattan Independent, August 10, 1863, February 1865.

Manhattan Standard, September 19, 1869, 1870.

Secondary Sources

Andreas, A. T., Compiler, History of the State of Kansas, Andreas, Chicago, 1883.

Connelley, William Elsey, Kansas and the Kansans, Lewis Publishing Company, Chicago, 1918.

Connelley, William Elsey, History of Kansas Newspapers, Kansas State Printing Plant, Topeka, 1916.

Kansas Historical Collections, Vols. IV, VII, XVII, compiled by the Kansas Historical Society, Topeka, 1876.

The following selections were used:

Byers, O. P., "When Railroading Outdid the Wild West Stories," Vol. XVII, pp. 339-340.

Goodnow, Isaac T., "Personal Reminiscences and Kansas 1855," Vol. IV, p. 245.

Humphrey, James, "The Country West of Topeka Prior to 1865," Vol. IV, p. 291.

Martin, George W., "The Territorial and Military Combine at Fort Riley," Vol. VII.

Prentice, Noble L., History of Kansas, Published by E. P. Green, Winfield, Kansas, 1899.

Robinson, Sara T. L., Kansas Its Interior and Exterior Life, Crosby, Nicholas and Company, Boston, Mass., 1856.

Wilder, Daniel Webster, Annals of Kansas, George W. Martin, Topeka, 1875.

Williamson, Harold Arthur, The Effect of Railroads on the Development of Kansas to 1870, Manhattan, Kansas, 1930.

CPSIA information can be obtained
at www.ICGtesting.com
Printed in the USA
BVHW041336070119
537213BV00013B/207/P

9 781528 125352